The

POWER

of

BLESSING

The POWER *of* BLESSING

How a Carefully Chosen Word Changes Everything

DAVID TIMMS

BETHANYHOUSE
MINNEAPOLIS, MINNESOTA

Published by Bethany House Publishers
11400 Hampshire Avenue South
Bloomington, Minnesota 55438

Bethany House Publishers is a division of
Baker Publishing Group, Grand Rapids, Michigan.

Printed in the United States of America

In keeping with biblical principles of creation stewardship, Baker Publishing Group advocates the responsible use of our natural resources. As a member of the Green Press Initiative, our company uses recycled paper when possible. The text paper of this book is comprised of 30% post-consumer waste.

g green press INITIATIVE

Library of Congress Cataloging-in-Publication Data

Timms, David.
    The power of blessing : how a carefully chosen word changes everything / David Timms.
      p. cm.
    Includes bibliographical references.
    Summary: "Explores Jesus' timeless words in the beatitudes and offers a framework for blessing others—and being blessed. Includes discussion questions for individual or group study"—Provided by publisher.
    ISBN 978-0-7642-0679-5 (pbk. : alk. paper) 1. Sermon on the mount—Criticism, interpretation, etc. I. Title.
    BT380.3.T56   2010
    226.9'306—dc22

2010016781

To Elizabeth Welch,
the mother of my best friend,
who has been a blessing
as long as I've known her.

Books by
David Timms

Living the Lord's Prayer

The Power of Blessing

Sacred Waiting

ACKNOWLEDGMENTS

Writing a book never happens in a vacuum, and this book is no exception. The words and concepts inevitably originate in the writings and teachings of others who have touched me over the years. And I'm blessed by the people who continue to support, instruct, correct, and encourage me. This book is really the fruit of their investment and our relationships.

I owe a great debt to those who meet regularly with me in formation groups; one in my home and two in the workplace. These groups include people earnest about their faith, whom the Lord uses to enlarge my faith and shape my life. Thanks first to each of you—Keith & Tracey Akiyama, Kevin & Darcy Flye, Scott & Stephanie Rosner, Don & Sonia Gerdts, Gary & Carol Tucker, Rob & Shannon Cogswell, Lind Coop, Chris Davis, Mary Wright, Cori DeWitt, Penny Garcia, Joyce Allan, Kayla McGill, Amy Merget, Sandee Venegas, Annette Mativo, Carol Davidson, and Brad Overholser.

I am also deeply grateful for the untiring, insightful, and expert help of my editor, Ellen Chalifoux. This is our third book together, and each experience has been a joy. Thanks, Ellen.

My dear friends Scott, Stephanie, and Rob worked through early drafts of the book and offered helpful feedback. Thanks for your suggestions and commitment to this project. You've each made a difference.

But none of this could have happened without the constant inspiration and encouragement of my family. Kim pored over the manuscript with loving attention, and her wisdom touches many pages. She and our three sons (Matthew, Caleb, and Joel) are an indescribable blessing from the Lord. I love each of you dearly.

Finally—and most important—I'm indebted beyond words to Christ, though He would graciously not consider me indebted at all. But for His grace, provision, companionship, transforming power, and guidance, there'd be nothing to say. To Him be all glory and honor, now and forevermore.

CONTENTS

The Power of Blessing

Words matter.

A single phrase or sentence can change a life. When a man and woman say to each other, "I do," it catapults them into an entirely new relationship. When a judge declares, "Not guilty!" those words produce enormous relief for the accused. When a firing-squad commander calls out, "Ready. Aim. Fire!" the blindfolded prisoner flinches for the last time. When the boss calls you in to say, "We're letting you go," everything changes.

Joel, my youngest son, enjoyed playing Little League baseball. During one season he struggled with confidence each time he came up to bat and frequently struck out without swinging. In his last at-bat of that season, his older brother Matthew—who was sitting on the bleachers watching the game—bellowed out "Swing!" just as the pitcher released the ball. His voice carried to the next county. Joel swung hard, connected with the ball, and sent it sailing into the outfield for a base hit. A single word from someone he trusted turned the end of the season into a victory celebration.

This book addresses, in part, the most powerful and life-changing tools at our disposal—words. These simple sounds, expressed in a particular way or order, powerfully shape us whether we hear them in an office cubicle, at a meal table, on the phone, or out on a baseball diamond.

POSITIVE, NEGATIVE, AND NEUTRAL

Our words fall into three basic categories: positive, negative, and neutral. For the most part, our lives include a lot of words in each category, though negativity tends to dominate.

In 2004, Robert Schrauf, an associate professor of applied linguistics and an anthropologist at Pennsylvania State University, did a study of adults in Mexico City and Chicago. "I found this surprising result," Schrauf says. "Half of all the words that people produce from their working vocabulary to express emotion are negative. Thirty percent are positive and 20 percent are neutral."[1] These proportions held true across cultural and generational lines.

Not only must we deal with the proliferation of negative language, but psychologists tell us that the power of a negative word is exponentially greater than the power of a positive word. Dr. John Gottman, at the University of Washington, says that the ratio of positive to negative words should be five-to-one for married couples, because negativity sticks harder and longer than affirmation.[2]

But if negative words have an enormous power in our lives, carefully chosen and timely positive words can have the same.

Mary Ann Bird's personal story, recounted in *The Whisper Test*, highlights the life-changing power of positive words. She was born with multiple birth defects: deaf in one ear, a cleft palate, a disfigured face, a crooked nose, and lopsided feet. As a child, she dreaded other children staring at her and asking the embarrassing question: "What happened to your lip?"

"I cut it on a piece of glass," she would lie.

Each year the children had their hearing tested at school. The classroom teacher would call each child to the front desk and have the child cover first one ear, and then the other. The teacher would then whisper some simple phrase to the child, such as, "The sky is blue" or "You have new shoes." This was the whisper test. If the child could repeat the phrase, then their hearing was apparently fine and they passed the test. To avoid humiliation, Mary Ann always cheated on the test, casually cupping her hand over her one good ear so that she could hear what the teacher said.

One year, Mary Ann's classroom teacher was Miss Leonard, one of the most loved and popular teachers in the school. She exuded gentleness and loved the children deeply. When the time came for Mary Ann's hearing test, Mary Ann cupped her hand over her good ear as she had done so many times before and strained to hear what Miss Leonard would whisper. "I waited for those words," Mary Ann wrote, "that God must have put into her mouth; those seven words that changed my life." Miss Leonard did not say, "The sky is blue" or "You have new shoes." She whispered, *"I wish you were my little girl."* And those seven positive, powerful words became a watershed moment in Mary Ann Bird's life.[3]

> Nothing really changed for Mary Ann Bird. She remained disfigured and deaf in one ear and the object of her classmates' painful ridicule. But everything changed for Mary Ann Bird. She began to see that her classmates' judgments were neither the only words about her nor the final words. She started to understand herself as loved and lovable and dared to envision a future not constrained by her circumstances but a future that could transcend them. Indeed, following in the footsteps of the teacher who set her free, Mary Ann Bird herself became an acclaimed teacher known for her compassion and kindness.[4]

GOD-GIVEN, LIFE-SHAPING WORDS

Mary Ann Bird's experience comes as little surprise to anyone who reads the Bible. Words have always held sacred, God-touched, grace-filled, life-producing potential. Indeed, the first recorded blessing in human history comes from God himself in the garden of Eden.

After creating Adam and Eve, "God *blessed* them; and God *said* to them, 'Be fruitful and multiply, and fill the earth, and subdue it' " (Genesis 1:28 NASB). We shouldn't understand this as a mandate but as an opportunity. God's blessing made procreation, habitation, and dominion possible and positive. Without His blessing, these things become difficult, twisted, and even burdensome.

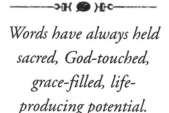

Words have always held sacred, God-touched, grace-filled, life-producing potential.

When God extended to us the gift of communication, He intended it primarily for the sacred task of building, nurturing, and deepening relationships with others. In a fallen world, however, we more often use words for personal gain or to threaten, intimidate, teach, set goals, or produce. But language that ends there stops short of the divine model. Words that serve only to inform or entertain fail their foundational purpose.

Language is not an evolutionary development but a divine gift for community. It has not arisen accidentally in the course of human history. Rather it initiated human history. God spoke everything into being, and His words not only created life but they continue to extend love and grace. His words—and ours—have a sacred and sacramental quality.

Of course, no one teaches us more about the power of words and blessings than Jesus himself. Even in the first few chapters of Mark's gospel, we see it over and over. When a leper came to Jesus begging for healing, Jesus *said,* "I am willing. Be clean" (Mark 1:41). When a paralyzed man was lowered through a roof to Him, Jesus *said,* "Son, your sins are forgiven" (Mark 2:5). When Jesus encountered a demon-possessed man near the Sea of Galilee, He *said,* "Come out of this man, you evil spirit!" (Mark 5:8). When a woman, afflicted with a bleeding problem for twelve years, touched the hem of Jesus' garment to be healed, He *said,* "Daughter, your faith has healed you. Go in peace and be freed from your suffering" (Mark 5:34).

Healing, deliverance, and freedom became reality with these words of Jesus. His words imparted grace in a world devoid of it and desperately needing it.

BLESSINGS IN THE ANCIENT WORLD

Men and women of all cultures throughout human history have known the power of a blessing (a "good word") to change a life.[5] In the ancient world, blessings—largely overlooked and seldom expressed in our day—could turn a life around.

Over the centuries, Jews have traditionally greeted each other with *shalom*—a term that loosely translates as "peace." The term, however, is not just a greeting but an invocation: "May God grant you peace, goodwill, good health, prosperity, and well-being in every way."[6]

In ancient Israel, the Lord told the priests to bless the sons of Israel by *saying* to them:

> The LORD bless you and keep you; the LORD make his face shine upon you and be gracious to you; the LORD turn his face toward you and give you peace. (Numbers 6:24–26)

And the Lord added, "So they shall invoke My name on the sons of Israel, and I then will bless them" (v. 27 NASB). The priests spoke these words loudly and publicly, calling on God. And the words prompted action and produced a new reality. Blessing someone was a prophetic act.

When the Old Testament patriarchs faced their own deaths they would commonly gather their sons together and pronounce a blessing—not as wishful thinking but with the conviction that carefully chosen words would produce real results.[7] The blessings established a covenant between the patriarch, the son, and God.

And since God himself would not die, the blessing was bound to be fulfilled.

In the first century, at the time of Jesus, Jewish mothers would ask local rabbis to speak a blessing over their children. Indeed, Mark records, "People were bringing little children to Jesus to have him touch them . . . and he took the children in his arms, put his hands on them and blessed them" (Mark 10:13, 16). The Jews knew that God created the world with words. He didn't squeeze the planets into shape with His hands. He *said*, "Let there be . . ." and there was. From the very beginning of time, words have created, produced, shaped, and blessed.

We find this idea of blessings expressed in every culture. Even in Western culture today we often greet each other with "Good morning" or something similar. Perhaps without realizing it, we speak a word of blessing as an echo of an ancient conviction that such words have the capacity to help shape someone else's experience. As we say, "Good morning," we dare to speak goodness into being for the other person.

Every culture formulates words in traditional ways and passes them down from generation to generation, words of life as well as words of death. But always words. Yet even the most powerful words can slowly suffocate and lose their impact, and the farther we travel from Eden, the less confidence we have in the creative capacity of our words.

THE DEMISE OF THE WORD

Words without application lack power. Constant speech without significance sucks the life out of our language. To speak *about* rather than to speak *to* violates the fundamental purpose of language. To *use* words but not *live* words incapacitates them.

Parker Palmer, a renowned educator and author, discovered this in his own life. As a university professor, he hit a painful period in his career when words just seemed to dry up—a disaster for a prolific speaker and writer. He struggled to attend his classes, to speak, or to write anything. And for nearly two years he grew increasingly desperate, angry, and despondent—and abandoned his university career. Sometime later he looked back with better understanding.

To speak about *rather than to speak* to *violates the fundamental purpose of language.*

> Now I see the deeper lesson my experience was meant to teach. Words began to fail me because I was not following them with my life. I was failing to incarnate what truth I had been given, and my words, lacking flesh, were skeletons with no animation or powers of regeneration. Only as I began to act on the social concerns I had spoken about in class, only as I began trying to live the vision of community I had once written about, did my words begin to return.[8]

Words, intended for blessing and life, have suffered a dreadful demise in our day. They fill time slots and pages rather than lives. They push aside uncomfortable silences. They amuse and distract us and have lost much of their vigor through misuse and overuse.

Jacques Ellul, a renowned French philosopher, describes it as "the humiliation of the word." He writes:

> No one consciously tried to bring it about, yet the situation of the word in our society is deplorable. . . . The habit of speaking without saying anything has eaten away at the word like a cancer. . . . Instead of limiting ourselves to what is useful (no more and no less) for exchanging information, news, and teaching, we keep on speaking. . . . These days we speak without saying anything; we just chitchat. . . .
> In spite of the lack of anything to say, the speaker continues as if he were a word-mill moved by the wind, and he becomes responsible for the fact that no one can any longer take *any* word

seriously. *No* word can be taken seriously, because the rush of these words prevents us from discovering the one which, in the midst of the torrent, has meaning and deserves to be listened to.[9]

In such an environment, we desperately need the reprise of blessings. We need to restore the ancient understanding of words. The power of words needs revival. And as we consider a renaissance of blessings, we have no better teacher than Jesus. Yet the blessings that Jesus uttered strike us as contrary to the soft, affirming, everything-will-be-all-right platitudes that we commonly hear.

THE BLESSINGS OF JESUS

As we've already noted, blessings were sought, exchanged, and deeply valued in the first century. Thus the opening words of Jesus' Sermon on the Mount (Matthew 5–7) carried special weight. As He opened His mouth, His first word was "Blessed." It surely caught everyone's attention. Who will be blessed? What will the blessing be?

"Blessed are the poor in spirit. . . . Blessed are those who mourn. . . . Blessed are the meek. . . . Blessed are those who hunger and thirst for righteousness. . . . Blessed are the merciful. . . . Blessed are the pure in heart. . . . Blessed are the peacemakers. . . . Blessed are those who are persecuted because of righteousness. . . ."

There's a blessing for those who are beaten, abandoned, down-and-out, hurt, weak, discouraged, disillusioned, and oppressed.

These blessings strike us as very odd. On the one hand, they sound like good news—especially for those who are beaten, abandoned, down-and-out, hurt, weak, discouraged, and oppressed. On the other hand, the blessings completely invert the cultural norms of Jesus' day and ours. We expect Him to declare the middle-class mantras of our time:

"Blessed are the wealthy, for they have everything they need."

"Blessed are the healthy, for they will prevail in the struggle for survival."

"Blessed are the educated, for their knowledge gives them superior leverage."

"Blessed are the powerful, for they call the shots."

"Blessed are the famous, for they always have admirers."

But Jesus sees greater blessing in qualities we usually dismiss or avoid. And in eight short couplets—just seventy-two words in the original Greek language—Jesus lays out blessings that provide deep insight into the abundant life and the Kingdom of God. His blessings take us by surprise because He does not attach prosperity or power to them. He speaks blessing to the marginalized of society, and those blessings focus more on the heart of the recipient than on their circumstances. And in those few compact words, Jesus casts a vision for the Kingdom of God that completely contradicts what we teach and expect in the kingdoms of this world.

In more recent times, Brennan Manning has written words that have a similar effect. In opening his bestselling book, he writes:

The Ragamuffin Gospel was written for the bedraggled, beat-up, and burnt-out.

It is for the sorely burdened who are still shifting the heavy suitcase from one hand to the other.

It is for the wobbly and weak-kneed who know they don't have it all together and are too proud to accept the handout of amazing grace.

It is for inconsistent, unsteady disciples whose cheese is falling off their cracker.

It is for poor, weak, sinful men and women with hereditary faults and limited talents.

It is for earthen vessels who shuffle along on feet of clay.

It is for the bent and the bruised who feel that their lives are a grave disappointment to God.

It is for smart people who know they are stupid and honest disciples who admit they are scalawags.[10]

The gospel of grace has always been for such people, and Jesus proclaimed the Beatitudes for the same such people, though biblical scholar and author Andrej Kodjak suggests that His opening of the Sermon on the Mount was designed to shock the audience as a deliberate inversion of standard values.[11] Perhaps as we explore these Beatitudes they'll prove as much a shock to us as to anyone over the past twenty centuries.[12] But these blessings—as unusual as they may sound—will strengthen, renew, and shape us positively.

If we could restore the status of blessings in our day—Kingdom blessings—our lives might change dramatically. May our journey into these ancient blessings—the blessings of the Beatitudes—be life-giving and life-changing for us.

SUMMARY STATEMENT

Our words have the God-touched power to shape lives. Men and women throughout the ages have understood this and spoken blessings with care and intentionality. Jesus did the same and chose to open His renowned Sermon on the Mount with a series of unexpected (and unusual) blessings.

Discussion Questions

1. What have been some of the most positive life-shaping words that you've received? And how have they affected your life?

2. Read James 3:7–10. What steps can we take to better "tame the tongue"?

3. The chapter suggests that "to speak *about* rather than to speak *to* violates the fundamental purpose of language."

How much of our language is informational? How might we modify our language to make it more relational?

4. What did you find most helpful in the introduction, and how can you apply it to your life in the next few days?

CHAPTER 1

Blessed Are the Poor in Spirit

"Blessed are the poor in spirit,
for theirs is the kingdom of heaven."

Janet wanted a blessing. She was a member of the Daybreak community in Toronto, which serves people with significant developmental disabilities. So she approached Henri—the community priest and pastor—and asked, "Henri, can you give me a blessing?" Somewhat ritualistically and a little insensitively, Henri traced the sign of the cross on her forehead with his thumb.

"No, that doesn't work!" exclaimed Janet. "I want a real blessing."

Suddenly, Henri realized how disconnected he had been. "Oh, I am sorry," he said. "Let me give you a real blessing when we are all together for the prayer service."

After the prayer service, Henri mentioned to the thirty or so people gathered there that Janet would like a blessing. And before he could say much more, she had quickly left her place and walked up to him. He was wearing a long white robe with full sleeves, consistent with his Roman Catholic priesthood, and Janet spontaneously wrapped her arms around him and put her head on his chest.

Henri, without thinking, wrapped his arms around her and she virtually vanished in the folds of his robe. Then he spoke some carefully considered words: "Janet, I want you to know that you are God's beloved daughter. You are precious in God's eyes. Your beautiful smile, your kindness to the people in your house, and all the good things that you do show us what a beautiful human being you are. I know you feel a little low these days and that there is some sadness in your heart, but I want you to remember who you are: a very special person, deeply loved by God and all the people who are here with you."

When Henri finished these few words of blessing, Janet raised her head and looked at him. A broad smile broke out across her face. She had heard and received the blessing.[1] Janet, one of the "least of these" by the world's standards, received a word, a personal word that gave her hope and sustained her soul.

THE ANCIENT BLESSINGS

The crowd that gathered around Jesus on that Galilean hillside came to hear good news. They had seen Him heal the sick and cast out demons (Matthew 4:24), and a buzz filled the air. For the most part, these people were the marginalized, the outcast, the hurt, the wounded, the forgotten, the neglected, and the underclass of Jewish society. The Pharisees called these common folk "sinners" because of their inability or reluctance to live up to strict religious standards. The religious leaders tolerated them at best, preferring to avoid them, and made it clear that these spiritually incompetent individuals were the reason for Israel's woes.[2]

Surrounded by these spiritual beggars, whose hearts were as famished as their stomachs, Jesus began to speak. And He spoke blessings before anything else.

> Blessed are the poor in spirit, for theirs is the kingdom of
>   heaven.
> Blessed are those who mourn, for they shall be comforted.
> Blessed are the gentle, for they shall inherit the earth.
> Blessed are those who hunger and thirst for righteousness,
>   for they shall be satisfied.
> Blessed are the merciful, for they shall receive mercy.
> Blessed are the pure in heart, for they shall see God.
> Blessed are the peacemakers, for they shall be called sons of
>   God.
> Blessed are those who have been persecuted for the sake of
>   righteousness, for theirs is the kingdom of heaven. (Mat-
>   thew 5:3–10 NASB)[3]

These words must have sounded as strange to the first-century hearers as they do to us. What's good about spiritual poverty? How is mourning beneficial? The gentle just get crushed. The pure in heart experience nothing but opposition and disillusionment. Who enjoys being persecuted? And as Jesus spoke these words, He likely looked around the crowd at specific people who belonged in each category; whose hopes and dreams felt dashed, whose best and purest intentions got trampled beneath the daily violence and their struggle for survival. Yet He promised them the Kingdom of heaven, the earth, comfort, mercy, and privileged status with God. How shall we make sense of these blessings?

THE WRONG APPROACH

We can easily misinterpret these ancient blessings and in the blink of an eye turn them from blessings to burdens.

Many readers might think that these eight Beatitudes prescribe *how to* enter the Kingdom of heaven, *how to* be satisfied (or fulfilled), *how to* inherit the earth, *how to* see God, *how to* become the sons of God, and so on. In other words, we misunderstand Jesus and conclude that His blessings flow from our fulfilling this new set of conditions. "If we could just be more broken, more grief-stricken, more persecuted, more . . . , then we'd be blessed."

This cannot be true. At least not in the sense that these qualities secure our place in the Kingdom of heaven or give us access to the Father's inheritance or the Father himself. From this distorted perspective, each "quality" becomes a way to qualify for a blessing and a means to attain God's favor. But this perspective has several obvious problems.

First, not all "poor in spirit" people are in the Kingdom. In fact, just the opposite, it seems that the Kingdom includes many very proud people. Similarly, not everyone who grieves is comforted. Some folk never really recover from the pain of a deep hurt or loss. Jesus must have had more in mind.

Second, if these are virtues for us to strive for, it simply encourages another form of "works righteousness," a way to earn the Lord's blessing. We do this; He owes us that.

> *The beatitudes do not reflect the only way to blessing but affirm that there is blessing for us irrespective of our circumstances.*

Third, we do not enter the Kingdom of heaven through means of spiritual poverty (the first beatitude) or persecution (the last beatitude). We know that we receive the Kingdom through faith in Christ.[4] The Beatitudes do not reflect the only way to blessing but affirm that there is blessing for us irrespective of our circumstances.

Dallas Willard, in his widely acclaimed book *The Divine Conspiracy*, suggests that our misunderstanding of the "blesseds" given by Jesus has "caused much pain and confusion down through the ages and continue[s] to do so today. . . . For many they have proved to be nothing less than pretty poison."[5] He goes on to say, "Those poor in spirit are called 'blessed' by Jesus, not because they are in a meritorious condition, but because, *precisely in spite of and in the midst of their ever so deplorable condition*, the rule of the heavens has moved redemptively upon and through them by the grace of Christ."[6] The Kingdom of God is available to all the "sat upon, spat upon, ratted on,"[7] not because of their circumstances but despite their circumstances. No one is beyond beatitude. And so we come to the first "blessed" on the lips of Jesus.

THE FIRST BEATITUDE

Blessed are the poor in spirit. The poor in spirit—those with neither spiritual pedigree nor spiritual achievements, the deprived and deficient, the spiritual beggars, those without a wisp of respectable religion—receive the Kingdom of heaven because they are with Jesus; accepted by Him, redeemed, forgiven, chosen, and changed. They have entrance to the Kingdom because they recognize their need and give their attention and allegiance to the King. Their circumstances don't matter a whit.

This provides the foundation on which we must approach each of the eight Beatitudes. The initial blessing of the Lord depends not on our religious or emotional state, nor on our efforts or attitudes, nor on our circumstances or situation, but on our connection to Him. If we receive blessing, it's because we've attached ourselves to Christ; we've responded to Him. The hopeless become the "blessed" by looking to Him.

As Brennan Manning notes, "The Kingdom belongs to people who aren't trying to look good or impress anybody, even themselves."[8] The poor in spirit to whom Jesus spoke that day could have access to the Kingdom of heaven because the King of heaven stood among them. Their spiritual failures and inadequacy did not preclude them from the Kingdom, because the King welcomed them despite their weaknesses—just as He welcomes us.[9]

Our Weakness—His Invitation

Dorothy Day, famous for her devotion to social justice and her influential editorial work on *The Catholic Worker*, quotes her mentor, Father John Hugo, who said, "Physical work was hard, mental work harder, and spiritual work was the hardest of all."[10] Many of us would agree. We often feel spiritually deficient. We don't pray as much or as well as we'd like to; don't read as frequently or as attentively as we should; don't serve others sufficiently; and don't generally engage in spiritual disciplines with any kind of regularity. Our "quiet times" often have the consistency of the wind and we share our faith with the intensity of cows at pasture. Deep within many of us lies a nagging awareness that we fail the spiritual test. Husbands carry a gnawing guilt as they struggle to offer spiritual leadership in their homes. Young dating couples, inflamed by their love, feel like spiritual failures as they cross the line of premarital intimacy with each other. Men and women who return to the church many years after moral failures, broken marriages, and wounded relationships frequently believe that their spiritual freefall now disqualifies them from spiritual leadership.

Spiritual work is the hardest of all.

The Kingdom of heaven belongs to us—not because of our virtue but because of Christ's.

Yet the timeless words of Jesus to the bedraggled gathering near the Galilean shoreline continue to speak loudly. The Kingdom of heaven belongs to us—not because of *our* virtue but because of Christ's. Our failings, weaknesses, mistakes, offenses, and spiritual inconsistencies neither qualify nor disqualify us from the Kingdom. Our faith is the issue. None of us can enter the Kingdom through any virtue of our own. None of us—not even those in a fifty-year marriage with saintly children and a track record of generosity, gentleness, and gratitude—can squeeze through the door on our own merit. In a nutshell, we must realize our need for God.

Jesus invites us all not on the basis of who *we* are but who *He* is. While some of us have managed the external exhibition of our sin more successfully than others, we share corrupt hearts in common. All of us have the potential (and propensity) to do the worst things. We may be sincere Lutheran believers mesmerized by a Hitler; Hutu Christians blinded by fear and a genocidal mob mentality; an emotionally susceptible leader suddenly alone with an attentive "other woman"; or financially stressed executives with access to the books. Time and again, the most genuine believers have proven vulnerable to the perfect storm. And only the ignorant or the deceived would assert otherwise. Spiritual destitution describes us all—apart from Christ.

Bill served as a deacon in a church that I pastored many years ago. His life story included tales of waywardness and brokenness, leaving the church as a rebellious youngster and then returning much later as a more subdued and broken man. He could happily serve the Communion elements and help out on church clean-up days, but when I approached him to lead the congregation in some devotional thoughts or in prayer he balked; not because he feared public speaking but because he considered himself ineligible for spiritual leadership. He had failed to keep up appearances throughout his life so he ruled himself out, oblivious to the fact (and unwilling to accept) that faith, not perfection, qualifies a person to receive the Kingdom of heaven. And, having received the Kingdom, we find ourselves entitled to all of its rights and privileges.

Thus, at the first level, the Beatitudes with which Jesus opens His extraordinary Sermon on the Mount remind us that neither brokenness, grief, hardship, nor any other life circumstance can keep us from the Kingdom of God—or the King himself.

But, as many writers have suggested, the Beatitudes carry a second level of significance for us. It is an invitation to live differently and to value what the world avoids: brokenness, grief, humility, mercy, purity, and peace.

A SECOND LEVEL

"Blessed are the poor in spirit, for theirs is the kingdom of heaven."

John Stott, typical of many commentators, writes, "The beatitudes are Christ's own specification of what every Christian ought to be. All these qualities are to characterize all his followers. . . . [They] describe his ideal for every citizen of God's kingdom."[11] I believe Stott stretches the text a little too far by making the Beatitudes *essential qualities* for every Christian, yet he is correct in identifying a secondary level within them that brings richness and wholeness to our lives.

Eugene Peterson paraphrases this opening beatitude with the words "You're blessed when you're at the end of your rope. With less of you there is more of God and his rule" (Matthew 5:3 THE MESSAGE). And he's right.

On the one hand, we affirm that spiritual poverty—the recognition that we are spiritually destitute and nothing without God—is not the means by which we inherit the Kingdom of God. On the other hand, without a sense of our continual spiritual need, we live with pride and self-sufficiency, which undermines our Kingdom living. Only spiritual beggars can have hearts attuned to the realities of grace. Spiritual smugness deadens us.

Who would have imagined that blessing lay "at the end of [our] rope"? Even more surprising—who would have imagined that this might be the starting place for "more of God and his rule"?

Poverty of spirit—brokenness—hardly attracts anyone. Yet until we reach this place of brokenness, the reign of God often remains distant and theoretical.

As Jesus launched His ministry, He visited His old stomping grounds in Nazareth—a place where He knew a lot of people and they knew Him. He entered the local synagogue, and they extended to Him the privilege of reading the Scripture that Sabbath morning. As it turned out, the attendant handed Jesus the scroll of the prophet Isaiah, and Jesus unrolled it to Isaiah 61 and began to read it out loud:

Until we reach the place of brokenness, the reign of God often remains distant and theoretical.

The Spirit of the Lord is on me, because he has anointed me to preach good news to the poor. He has sent me to proclaim freedom for the prisoners and recovery of sight for the blind, to release the oppressed, to proclaim the year of the Lord's favor. (Luke 4:18–19)

His mission, succinctly stated, was to proclaim good news to broken people—the poor, the prisoner, the blind, the oppressed, and the captive; people who had lost everything that mattered most—and restore their dominion, their freedom, and their sight.

The poor in spirit and the brokenhearted—those whose lives have reached the lowest ebbs imaginable—are best placed to receive Kingdom life if their hearts remain open to it. Furthermore, their "poverty" is not how they enter the kingdom, but it is how they live in it. And they live with a measure of humility, knowing that they deserve none of what the Father gives. And eventually this humility expresses itself not in self-absorption but in selfless service to others.

THE DOORSTEP OF HELL

Thomas Merton observed some decades ago in his book *No Man Is an Island*, "We cannot find Him unless we know we need Him. We forget this need when we take a self-sufficient pleasure in our own good works. The poor and helpless are the first to find Him, Who came to seek and to save that which was lost."[12] Much earlier in the book, he wrote, "To consider persons and events and situations only in the light of their effect upon myself is to live on the doorstep of hell."[13]

How ironic. We point to those who look stricken and humiliated and believe they may be furthest from the Kingdom. Yet in reality, those who are entirely self-absorbed stand on the doorstep of hell. It's so easy to look at *ourselves* in an economy that is reeling like a drunkard. Perhaps it's a pay cut, a job loss, or financial hardship. It's so easy to look at *our own pain* in a world filled with sickness, violence, and suffering. It's so easy to look at *our circumstances* when we feel victimized by unfairness and injustice.

Yet truthfully, to consider everything around us purely in light of its impact upon us is to descend into a level of self-centeredness and selfishness that not only distracts us from Christ but from real life itself. Such narcissism represents the polar opposite of being poor in spirit.

The tragic irony of selfishness is that as we strive to care more for ourselves and protect our own interests, we actually harm ourselves and lose what matters most. The more the world revolves around us, the smaller we and the world become. As we hold increasingly tightly to our own lives, we inevitably find that we're grasping nothing but air. Life is not to be held tightly but to be given freely. Similarly, we do not generate life but receive it from others.

Perhaps a meaningful definition of *hell* is "isolation from God and others." For the independent atheist this may sound idyllic, but nothing drains and destroys us faster.

Whatever tough times we may face, will we descend into the abyss of selfishness or look at others around us? Will we pity ourselves or trust Christ? Will we strive for attention or deflect it to others? Will we complain of our own circumstances or simply surrender them to Christ?

Merton does not call for a false stoicism, as though we ought to put on a brave face no matter what. Rather he rephrases these immortal words of Jesus: "Whoever wishes to save his life will lose it; but whoever loses his life for My sake will find it" (Matthew 16:25 NASB). This latter loss is no accident but a carefully calculated choice.

When the wheels are loose—in our workplace, in our marriage, in our church, in our own life—let's resolve not to shutter the windows but to open them; not to worry about our own interests but to minister to the hearts of others. In doing so, we may find that what looks like the doorstep of hell actually becomes a window to the Kingdom of heaven.

HUMILITY IN THE KINGDOM

Jesus starts His Kingdom manifesto—the Sermon on the Mount—by blessing the poor in spirit. Could any quality be more needed (and generally less desired) in our own day?

The apostle Paul urged the believers at Philippi with these words: "Don't push your way to the front; don't sweet-talk your way to the top. Put yourself aside, and help others get ahead. Don't be obsessed with getting your own advantage. Forget yourselves long enough to lend a helping hand" (Philippians 2:3–4 THE MESSAGE). Then Paul drove it home by telling his readers to look to the example of Christ, who emptied himself and took the form of a servant. James reminded his readers: "God opposes the proud but gives grace to the humble" (James 4:6), reiterating the ancient message of the psalmist that the Lord "regards the lowly, but the haughty He knows from afar" (Psalm 138:6 NASB).

―――――⇥⊰ ● ⊱⇤―――――

The chaos within us personally and within many churches today derives not from the struggle to defer to each other but to defeat each other.

―――――⇥⊰ ● ⊱⇤―――――

The chaos within us personally and within many churches today derives not from the struggle to defer to one another but to defeat one another. Division comes not as we seek to be servants but as we strive to be sovereigns. We highly value our own opinions, experiences, and education, and our self-satisfaction often produces condescending and patronizing attitudes. We could hardly describe this as humility or poverty in spirit.

But we must make a vital observation. Some may consider this call to humility to be a manipulative tool, a mechanism whereby the powerful subdue the masses and control the crowds. If we can guilt or shame people into silence or service, then they pose no threat of rebellion. But nothing could be further from Jesus' mind.

Humility is not an abject, defeated attitude. To the contrary, it recognizes the "divine image" in everyone and refuses to manipulate or exploit anyone. It springs from a profound sense of the Father's sovereignty and a deep trust in His provision and love. It sees life as bigger and more than "me" and dedicates itself to "us." It eschews the trivial honors that commonly divide us but respects all people for their greatest honor of all—being created in the image of God. And to the extent that we nurture this "poor in spirit" attitude we discover the secret of contentment and productivity and life that awaits us in the countercultural Kingdom of God.

"You're blessed when you're at the end of your rope. With less of you there is more of God and his rule" (Matthew 5:3 THE MESSAGE).

SUMMARY STATEMENT

Blessed are the poor in spirit, because Christ welcomes them into His Kingdom despite their lack of spiritual heritage and aptitude.

Indeed, their brokenness and humility usually make their hearts more sensitive to the Presence and reign of God and more receptive to His blessings.

Discussion Questions

1 Describe in your own words what it means to be poor in spirit.

2. Why do the poor in spirit (the broken and the humble) have an advantage in Kingdom living?

3. How does our brokenness lead to productiveness in the Kingdom of God?

4. What is your response to Merton's suggestion that "to consider persons and events and situations only in the light of their effect upon myself is to live on the doorstep of hell"?

CHAPTER 2

Blessed Are Those Who Mourn

"Blessed are those who mourn,
for they will be comforted."

Sue Mosteller tells the moving story of one of Henri Nouwen's first visits to the Daybreak community. Nouwen, whom I mentioned at the start of the last chapter, was a renowned Catholic priest, educator, writer, and speaker. Before he moved permanently to Daybreak, he had requested a place to stay at the community for ten days so he could cloister himself away and write intensively.

> After only a few days, Raymond, a member of the community with a disability, suffered a serious accident and was hovering between life and death in intensive care. Angry because of Daybreak's lack of proper supervision, the family forbade community members to visit Raymond at the hospital. Upon hearing this news, Henri borrowed a car and was met by Raymond's father in the waiting room connected to intensive care.
>
> "I am a priest," Henri said, "and I'm here to be with you and with Raymond. Tell me what is happening for your son and for

you." While Henri listened attentively, Raymond's father grieved his son's condition and expressed helplessness in the face of it. In time, Henri asked, "Have you blessed your son?"

Confused by the question, Raymond's dad replied, "No. Why? I don't understand what you are talking about. And I wouldn't even know where to begin."

Henri answered, "This is important. Come, I will help you. A father must bless his son. If Raymond dies, he will make that passage under your blessing, and if he lives, he will live with the blessing of his father. This is a very special thing to do."[1]

As Henri Nouwen guided that grieving parent to bless his son with words of affirmation, hope, love, and exhortation, the despair lifted. And with each word of blessing, the father's heart softened. Healing happened—spiritual healing—and forgiveness and reconciliation became possible. Nouwen told Raymond's dad that the whole Daybreak community was grieving his situation and felt anxious about Raymond. Finally he requested that the community come and visit Raymond. They were more than welcome. They were wanted. And the words that the father whispered in the ears of his suffering son that day became life-giving to both of them. The grief evoked an experience of love and intimacy that the everyday routine could not have.

GRIEF AND LOVE

Unless we are sociopaths or psychopaths, perhaps the most universal experience we share is grief. We grieve at losses of many kinds—a friend betrays us or abandons us, an ultrasound reveals no fetal movement, our supervisor hands us a pink slip, that small lump turns out to be a big deal, Alzheimer's steals the memories we once shared together. We all mourn. Sometimes we express it with quietness and a deep solitude of the soul. Other times we respond with weeping or anger or false bravado. We manifest grief in a variety of ways. And while some family or friends gently urge us to "get over it" or "move on" and counselors warn that we can "get stuck," grief grips and shapes us in powerful ways.

Behind much of our grief, not always but in many instances, lies love.[2] Indeed, grief often reflects a true tenderness of heart and a significant depth of love.

When a marriage fails, grief visits because the hopes and aspirations ignited by love have been quenched. When a friend dies, grief washes over us because we've lost someone we loved and someone who loved us, and the deeper that love the deeper our grief.

In simplest terms, those who fail to mourn do so because they have failed to love.

LeRoy Lawson writes: "After several years of pastoral ministry, I considered the alternative: 'Blessed are those who *don't* or *can't* mourn.' No, the hard-hearted and incapacitated are not blessed. They are deprived."[3]

Luke's gospel tells us that when Jesus approached the city of Jerusalem on one occasion he "wept over it" (Luke 19:41), deeply grieved at the hostility and harm that He knew the city would suffer. Such tears were the tears of love.

Those who fail to mourn do so because they have failed to love.

Jesus wept again when he came to the tomb of Lazarus and saw the grief of Mary and Martha and many others with them (John 11:35). He shared in their grief not out of a sense of social decorum or propriety, but because He loved them. Their pain produced pain within Him too. At the heart of it was love.

James Howell writes:

> The wisest book I have read on grief is *Lament for a Son*, written by the Yale philosopher Nicholas Wolterstorff in the aftermath of the mountain-climbing death of his twenty-five-year-old son, Eric.

Several years after this horrible loss, Wolterstorff noticed that "the wound is no longer raw. But it has not disappeared. That is as it should be. If he was worth loving, he is worth grieving over. Grief is existential testimony to the worth of the one loved. . . . Every lament is a love-song."[4]

Perhaps few of us think of lament as a love song. But it is. The wailing of men, women, and children as they found the bodies of family members and friends under the concrete rubble of Port-au-Prince, Haiti, after the devastating earthquake on January 12, 2010, ultimately expressed the depth of their love. On the one hand, grief can wash over us like a surging tide. It incapacitates us. It feels like an enemy—but it is an affirmation: an affirmation of love, of sensitive hearts, of the divine nature within us.

Surely Jesus had some of this in mind as He pronounced the beatitude. "Blessed are those who mourn." Interestingly, Jesus utilizes the present tense. He says, "Blessed *are* those who mourn. . . ." We would more likely say, "Blessed *will be* those who mourn." We typically comfort each other with words that point to the future. "It will be okay. It will pass. Everything will get better. You will survive." Will, will, will. What a contrast to Jesus' emphasis. "You *are* blessed, even as you mourn." In part, it's because we anticipate a comfort promised to all those who enter the Kingdom of heaven. But the mourning also declares something about our hearts in the present moment that we ought not to diminish.[5]

Robert Frost, famous twentieth-century American poet, finished his poem "Reluctance" with these words:

> Ah, when to the heart of man
> Was it ever less than treason
> To go with the drift of things,
> To yield with a grace to reason,
> And bow and accept the end
> Of a love or a season?[6]

As we begin to understand that laments are literally love songs, we see that mourning is evidence of that love. How blessed are those whose hearts love so deeply.

GRIEF AND REPENTANCE

While grief may reflect a tender heart, biblically it may also demonstrate a repentant one. Shame can produce mourning, and some tears are those of repentance, recognition that we have wounded the heart of God and offended the righteousness of God.

In the Old Testament, such contrition was typically expressed by wearing sackcloth and throwing ashes over oneself. Job declared, "I . . . repent in dust and ashes" (Job 42:6). The king of Nineveh, under conviction of his sin and God's pending judgment upon his city, "covered himself with sackcloth and sat on the ashes" (Jonah 3:6 NASB). Ezra and the people of Israel wept bitterly and lay prostrate before the house of God (Ezra 10:1). Jesus said that Tyre and Sidon "would have repented long ago in sackcloth and ashes" (Matthew 11:21). The apostle Paul groaned about his own sense of wretchedness (Romans 7:24), and he spoke very directly to the Corinthian believers when he wrote, "You have become arrogant and have not mourned instead [over your sin]" (1 Corinthians 5:2 NASB).

Many commentators point to sorrow for sin as the main focus of this beatitude,[7] or even its sole focus.[8] Yet while this godly sorrow produces a heart desire for change, we might also consider a deeper dynamic at work.

Is not this grief the fruit of the convicting work of the Holy Spirit within us?[9] Does not this sorrow arise from a spiritual awareness that we do not generate of ourselves, but which responds to the promptings and grace of the Holy Spirit within us? If so, then at the deepest levels our sorrow for sin affirms the grace of God toward us. And we are blessed to even have such sorrow. Without it, we would not truly repent. Without it, we would not turn toward

Christ. And therefore, without it we would have no fellowship with the Father, no intimacy with the Son, no guidance from the Holy Spirit. In short, we would have no salvation. Yes, indeed, blessed are those who mourn over their sin and shame, not because the tears have any redemption in them, but because they give testimony to the gracious stirring, calling, and convicting work of God's Spirit in our life.

The hardness of heart that afflicted the ancient Pharaoh (Exodus 7:13, 22; 8:15, 19, 32; 9:7, 12, 34–35), and so many men and women since, is not evidence of strength or courage. Far more tragically, it speaks of a heart insensitive to the voice of God and a quenched Holy Spirit.

> *Our mourning consistently affirms that Christ is being formed in us.*

Tears, typically seen as evidence of weakness or softness in our culture, mean just the opposite in the Kingdom of God. In the Kingdom, our mourning consistently affirms that Christ is being formed in us (Galatians 4:19).

Of course, some sorrow and mourning arise from simple immaturity and selfishness—the child who cries over a skinned knee, the teenager who weeps over a failed exam, or the tears that we shed when we can't have our way. But Jesus is hardly affirming such superficial or distorted causes. Those who grieve out of conviction or love are blessed in the very experience of mourning because their hearts are a breath away from the very heart of God himself.

Thomas Merton, much-loved for his profound and insightful spiritual writing, suggests that the mourning to which Jesus refers effectively washes away all the pretension and the flimsy pieces of emotional furniture within us that keep our souls from being utterly purged and from being fully ushered into the Presence of God. The tears function like torrential rain on a parched landscape, refreshing the air and catching up all the trash in the dry creeks and riverbeds and washing them away on turbulent waters.

> "Blessed are they that mourn." Can this be true? Is there any greater wretchedness than to taste the dregs of our own insufficiency and misery and hopelessness, and to know that we are certainly worth nothing at all? Yet it is blessed to be reduced to these depths if, in them, we can find God. Until we have reached the bottom of the abyss, there is still something for us to choose between all and nothing. There is still something in between. We can still evade the decision. When we are reduced to our last extreme, there is no further evasion.[10]

HIS DISTRESSING DISGUISE

Another element of mourning deserves our attention. The ancient Greeks called it *splanchnon*—a term commonly translated "compassion" or "longing." It's what Jesus felt when he looked at the leper (Mark 1:41). It's what the apostle Paul felt when he thought of the poverty-stricken but super-generous Macedonians in Philippi (Philippians 1:8). It's actually what Paul urges all of us to put on (Colossians 3:12). The term refers to the bowels of a person—that deep stirring of the gut that accompanies the deepest sympathy. It's grief over the suffering of others; compassion for the wounds and hurts we see in others. And we might feel this way for two reasons—the love of Christ within us and the recognition of Christ within them.

Mother Teresa was one such person. This small Albanian-born woman dedicated her life to serving the homeless, the oppressed, and the outcast in India. She felt compelled by a deep conviction that Christ *could* be found and *would* be found among the poor. "[We] help the poorest of the poor . . . which is always Christ in His distressing disguise."[11]

Her words echoed the plea of seventeenth-century Jesuit priest

Peter Claver, who ministered to the wounded, broken, and brutalized African slaves when their seaborne hellholes arrived in Colombia, South America. On one occasion, as Claver's helpers turned to flee from the gruesome spectacle of sickness and injury, he cried out to them, "It is Christ."[12]

Our view of the poor, the homeless, the marginalized, the abused, the beaten, and the crushed is often paternalistic. We don't mourn for their plight. Instead we criticize it—and them. "If they would just . . ." "Don't they know that . . . ?" "Why don't they . . . ?" Our condescension and complacency distances us from their need, and we tend to respond with increasing indifference, disinterest, or disgust. No tears. No sadness. No compassion.

Overwhelmed by the magnitude of the need around us, we toss a few dollars here and there, and then complain about corruption, laziness, irresponsible life choices, and failures—theirs.

And from time to time (very occasionally), just enough to assuage an irritating pang of conscience, we support a charitable cause and ride high on our generosity for a season.

Of course, not all of us are so callous or so hardened.

Some softer hearts and more sensitive spirits find themselves deeply moved by the injustice and brokenness of our world. They pour themselves out with varying degrees of abandon. They serve and sacrifice for the forgotten and the sidelined. They reach out with love and hope. After all, Jesus died for the afflicted and the neglected.

But how might we *all* change, how might we *all* respond if we saw the down-and-out, the disheveled, the disheartened, the dispossessed, and the dishonored through the lens of the gospel?

It is Christ . . . in distressing disguise.

Jesus told His disciples: "To the extent that you did it to one of these brothers of Mine, even the least of them, you did it to Me" (Matthew 25:40 NASB). Not *for* Me, but *to* Me.

Perhaps when we want to see Jesus, we'd do well to look where we usually close our eyes . . . and our hearts. He sits in the slums and skid rows of this world. He lives in the hovels and the halfway houses. And when we mourn for the brokenness and fallenness of the world around us, we share in the sufferings of Christ. We share His broken heart. And we are blessed.

Christ sits in the slums and skid rows of this world. He lives in the hovels and the halfway houses.

SITTING WITH HIM

Teresa, a co-worker of mine, used to sit on the front porch with her dad, until he passed away in 2009. He suffered from ALS (Lou Gehrig's disease)—a debilitating and degenerative disease. Those early evenings were filled with a grief of their own as the two of them sat and rocked on the swing together. He could not speak, but in the silence he imparted warmth and love to her; apart from words and apart from actions—with just his gentle, unassuming, reassuring presence. Teresa felt her grief comforted by his mere presence.

How often does the Father desire the same from us?

We have grown so accustomed to speech and action, to fixing and helping, to counseling and therapy, to busyness and distraction in the midst of our grief that we've perhaps forgotten that stillness and Presence—His Presence—ministers powerfully as we mourn.

The porch swing sits idle.

In the opening chapters of the apostle Paul's letter to the Ephesians, we read some of the loftiest theology in the New Testament. Paul's description of God's plan through Christ from the beginning of eternity is unparalleled. His prayer for the Ephesians at the end of the first chapter is extraordinary and powerful. Yet despite all of the ten-dollar words (*holy, blameless, heavenly realms, adoption, redemption, mystery, inheritance, revelation,* and so many more), Paul's million-dollar concept is wrapped up in a tiny, almost overlooked term—the word *with*. We barely notice it. We surely undervalue it. Yes, Paul describes the grace of God in powerful terms—saving us and resurrecting us to new life. But that new life is a "with" life. We've been made alive together "*with* Christ" (Ephesians 2:5) and raised up "*with* Christ" and seated "*with* him in the heavenly realms" (2:6).

We'd like to rewrite it just a tad. We'd generally prefer to simply be made alive, raised, and seated. No *with*.

But *with* is a gospel word. It signifies the very intention of the cross. It expresses the eternal purpose of God. He does not redeem us to build an army of workers, but to draw us back into His Presence; the Presence from which Adam and Eve fled.

—————⇥❨ ● ❩⇤—————

Those who mourn understand the value of simple presence—"withness."

—————⇥❨ ● ❩⇤—————

In our world, *with* seems only to have value when we are "working with," "competing with," or "speaking with," not merely "being with." But perhaps if we understood the degenerative disease we all carry called *sin,* we'd sit more humbly, more silently, and more appreciatively *with* the Father. And as we take in the brokenness and pain of the world around us we'd see Christ *with* us in the worst of circumstances.

Jesus cued us to this reality when He said, "I am *with* you always, even to the end of the age" (Matthew 28:20 NKJV). Matthew closes his gospel account with that all-important statement by Jesus. Jesus did not declare "I *toil* with you always" or "I *speak* with you always" but "I *am with* you always."

Just being together.

Those who mourn are blessed because they come to understand the value of simple presence—"withness."

Jesus looked at the ragtag crowd that surrounded him on that hillside and certainly surprised them. "Blessed are those who mourn, for they shall be comforted." We need not completely spiritualize the saying. Tears are tears. Grief is grief. But those who mourn are indeed blessed because:

- Authentic grief grounded in loss speaks to a heart of love
- Authentic grief grounded in shame bears testimony to the gracious work of God within us
- Authentic grief grounded in the suffering of others opens the door for us to see Christ
- Authentic grief that drives us into the places of solitude and aloneness allows us to sit *with* Christ as never before
- Authentic grief will one day be comforted with the comfort that only the Father supplies (2 Corinthians 1:3–5)

Such grief is far from destructive. It lays a foundation for our deepest formation.

"You're blessed when you feel you've lost what is most dear to you. Only then can you be embraced by the One most dear to you" (Matthew 5:4 THE MESSAGE).

SUMMARY STATEMENT

Those who mourn are blessed because they have a heart of love and understand the power of "presence." Thus they understand something of the heart of God. Furthermore, when repentance for our sin causes grief, we experience forgiveness, and when the brokenness of the world breaks our hearts, we may see Christ in His "distressing disguise."

Discussion Questions

1. How does understanding lament as love song help you approach grief?

2. Can we experience true repentance without a sense of mourning or sorrow?

3. How do you feel about the suggestion that those who suffer in the world might be "Jesus in His distressing disguise"? And what might you do to respond?

4. Those who mourn are blessed because they come to understand the value of simple presence—"withness," or being with someone. Can you identify with this statement?

CHAPTER 3

Blessed Are the Meek

*"Blessed are the meek,
for they will inherit the earth."*

Kevin Harney wrote thousands of notes. Six days a week for many years he sent out three handwritten notes of encouragement and blessing to people in the churches that he pastored.

One Sunday a volunteer on the church's sound-and-lighting team caught him after the worship service. In Kevin's words:

> This guy looks like Jesse "The Body" Ventura (the former professional wrestler and governor of Minnesota). He is a strong, self-assured, man's man. With tenderness in his eyes he looked at me and said, "Pastor, I need to tell you something. Over the years you have written me a number of notes telling me how God has used me and how much God loves me. I have kept every one of them. I keep them in a box at home. When I get discouraged and wonder if God can really do something with my life, I take out those notes and read them. I just thought you should know!"[1]

Kevin Harney had steadily built a culture of blessing in that church. He understood the ancient proverb "Words kill, words give life; they're either poison or fruit—you choose" (Proverbs 18:21 THE MESSAGE). And words of blessing touch the hearts of those with even the most hardened exterior.

Long before Kevin started writing his notes, Jesus used His words to encourage and motivate people. And as He surveyed the crowd gathered around Him on that first-century Galilean hillside, He pronounced a blessing on another group of listeners.

"Blessed are the meek, for they will inherit the earth."[2]

The meek? Jesus uses a fairly unusual word—the Greek word *praus*—an adjective found only a few other times in the New Testament. He would later describe himself as "meek (*praus*) and lowly in heart" (Matthew 11:29 KJV). Decades later, the apostle Peter urged Christian wives not to place their confidence in externals such as braided hair and jewelry but in the lasting beauty of "a meek (*praus*) and quiet spirit" (1 Peter 3:4 KJV).[3]

Given that Jesus uses this term to describe himself, we can hardly imagine that it speaks of a weak, indecisive, or fearful character. This word (sometimes translated *humble* or *gentle*) is a virtue that Christ honors—and considers *blessed*.

W. E. Vine provides helpful insight into the meaning of this unusual term:

[Meekness] is an inwrought grace of the soul; and the exercises of it are first and chiefly toward God. It is that temper of spirit in which we accept His dealings with us as good, and therefore without disputing or resisting. . . . The meaning of *prautēs* is not readily expressed in English, for the terms *meekness* [and] *mildness* . . . suggest weakness and pusillanimity to a greater or less extent, whereas *prautēs* does nothing of the kind. Described negatively, meekness is the opposite of self-assertiveness and self-interest; it is equanimity of spirit that is neither elated nor cast down, simply because it is not occupied with self at all.[4]

Those who are meek operate from a deep faith in the sovereignty of God. They have a security and contentment that allows them to feel no need to defend themselves or fight for "their rights." They may well advocate for the welfare and rights of others, but not for themselves. They do not display strong self-assertiveness and generally present themselves as level-headed and easygoing. That in itself makes meekness a rare trait in our culture. Yet we ought not underestimate or downplay the significance of the meek spirit.[5]

The meek operate from a deep faith in the sovereignty of God.

Consider a couple of examples of meekness in action.

At work, Jeff's company decided to restructure. He had worked for the company for fifteen years as a divisional leader, but when the senior management put together a task force to examine the restructure possibilities, they did not include him. Some of us would respond with hurt and negativity. But meekness doesn't mind. Nor does it complain, gossip, backbite, or whine.

Some onlookers, of course, might interpret Jeff's silence or reluctance to demand his rights as a sign of weakness. Our culture often equates aggressiveness and assertiveness with strength. But biblically, the silence of Christ on the cross demonstrates a much greater amount of strength than, for example, the whining of James and John about having privileged places in the coming Kingdom.

In another example, Amanda had often sung solos in the worship services at her church. She had a good voice and enjoyed serving in that way. But a new worship pastor arrived and decided to alter the worship format substantially. He rarely scheduled solos at all, and when they came along he assigned them to other folk he had befriended. Could we resist a complaining and critical spirit under such circumstances? But meekness does not grow bitter. Nor does it cause tension, dissension, or division.

This meekness evolves not from our natural selves. It only emerges through faith—deep faith—that the Father governs the very details of our lives.

THE MEEK MARKS

As you read this page, your eye picks up all the black letters. Those letters form the words that help you understand the message. But something else is critically important to your understanding—the small marks we call punctuation. We usually underrate them, but they make a world of difference. Consider a simple classic example of these "meek marks" in the following two sentences.

A woman, without her man, is nothing.

A woman: without her, man is nothing.

The meek marks have the power to completely change the meaning of a collection of words. Which of the following "Dear Jack" letters would you prefer to receive?

Dear Jack,

I want a man who knows what love is all about. You are generous, kind, thoughtful. People who are not like you admit to being useless and inferior. You have ruined me for other men. I yearn for you. I have no feelings whatsoever when we're apart. I can be forever happy—will you let me be yours? Jill

If we leave precisely the same words in place and change just the humble punctuation, we can reverse the message entirely.

Dear Jack,

I want a man who knows what love is. All about you are generous, kind, thoughtful people, who are not like you. Admit to being useless and inferior. You have ruined me. For other men I yearn! For you I have no feelings whatsoever. When we're apart I can be forever happy. Will you let me be? Yours, Jill[6]

Perhaps in a world of words, we'd like to be three syllables or more—strong words like *competent* or special words like *generous*. But the reality is that every word, much as it pops off a page, utterly depends for meaning and significance upon what we might call "the meek marks."

In the same way, Jesus announces that the meek are not nearly as useless or inferior as the world usually declares.[7] Just as punctuation makes a printed letter meaningful and silence between phrases or sentences gives significance and sense to what we say, so meekness—which seems destined to abuse or enslavement—actually paves the way to inherit the earth.

Jesus announces that the meek are not nearly as useless or inferior as the world usually declares.

Is it possible that followers of Jesus might serve as "meek marks" in the world? At times they may be underrated, understated, and underappreciated, but they always fulfill a powerful role in a world infatuated with size, power, and visibility. Godly parents who consistently pray for their children, support them, love them, and teach them the way of Jesus rarely receive public awards. Every encouraging text message, each word of affirmation (or correction) serves as a "meek mark" in a child's story or a friend's story. Do we trust Christ to gather together our seemingly insignificant efforts and shape lives with them? The meek do.

Of course, occasionally meekness stands out like an exclamation mark at the end of a sentence and people recognize and value it.

Mother Teresa functioned in such a way when she spoke with world leaders who vied to meet with her. She was the "meek mark" that gave focus and direction to the sophisticated, educated, and popular powers of her day. In fact, she liked to describe herself as a mere pencil in the hand of God.[8] Her life modeled deep humility and enormous influence, not because she sought influence but because she devoted herself to obedience. That's what the meek do.

Jesus calls us to such meekness, not because He desires to diminish us in any way but because, ironically, "the last shall be first" (Matthew 19:30 KJV) and the servant shall be the greatest (Mark 10:43–44). More than that, blessing awaits the meek and the gentle. Yet how we struggle to trust Christ and recede behind Him. We seek the limelight rather than shun it. We fear insignificance and therefore pursue prominence, to our detriment.

LOOK AT ME

In the early afternoon of October 15, 2009, national television stations broadcast startling images of a small homemade flying-saucer helium balloon racing dramatically out of control across the Colorado skies, thousands of feet above the ground.

Richard and Mayumi Heene created a media frenzy when they told emergency services personnel that their six-year-old son, Falcon, had climbed inside the balloon moments before it broke its tether in their backyard and drifted away. Within minutes millions of Americans were following the breaking story on television or radio, horrified by the possibilities. But when the balloon—losing helium through a weak seam or a puncture—finally landed in an open field, nobody was found inside, and attention turned back to the home.

Eventually it emerged that the Heenes had planned and perpetrated the hoax simply to generate publicity. They carefully orchestrated the entire charade to boost their chances of landing a television reality-show contract.[9] Such gratuitous self-promotion is shocking to most of us, and to manipulate your child for such self-serving ends seems unthinkable, yet it illustrates the extreme ends to which people go for a moment of fame and notoriety.

Far too often we want to attract attention rather than deflect it.

Yet we do the same thing, on a lesser scale. Far too often we want to attract attention rather than deflect it.

We drop hints about our titles, awards, achievements, successes, and even our spiritual disciplines. We may gently flaunt our biblical knowledge or carefully build a reputation for service intended to evoke gratitude from those we help or tell.

In short, we nurture a "look at me" Christianity.

Some of us are shameless in it, while others are subtle. But in the process of becoming "respectable sinners"—honorable in the eyes of those around us and honored by them—we forget that "we were dead in our transgressions" (Ephesians 2:5 NASB). According to the apostle Paul, the drug pusher, the pimp, the pastor, and the parishioner share a common death. And dead bodies have no meaningful distinction or attraction.

Yet Paul goes on to declare that "God . . . made us alive together with Christ" (Ephesians 2:4–5 ESV). We don't raise ourselves . . . and we don't live apart from Christ.

Our glory stories ought not to distract people from Jesus, but they often do. The accounts of fabulous turnarounds and miraculous changes can too easily leave people marveling at us rather than Him. Our testimonies tantalize our listeners briefly because of what He has done but mostly because of what we have become.

This "look at me" Christianity subtly distracts others from Jesus. Only as we *reckon* ourselves dead to sin and alive to Christ Jesus (and because of Christ and for Christ) will we become more like Him. Perhaps too often we criticize and judge others around us while at the same time doing the exact same negative things.

The meek need no attention. Meek not by circumstance but by choice, they have contentment. Humble in heart, they know the freedom that comes by releasing the need for power, fame, or success. Gentle in spirit, they experience the full blessing of being in the world but untouched by it. And while hardship may knock on their door and fear whisper in their ears, yet they have discovered the secret power of letting go of their agenda and trusting the Father's.

The apostle Paul urged the Colossian believers with these words: "Put on then, as God's chosen ones, holy and beloved, compassionate hearts, kindness, humility (*tapeinophrosune*), meekness (*prautēta*), and patience" (3:12). Notice that Paul uses two different terms—humility and meekness—and that this meekness arises from our conviction that we are the holy, beloved, chosen people of God. When this truth governs our hearts we can truly release our agenda and trust His.

PRIDE AND PRETENSE

A. W. Tozer once wrote, "The heart of the world is breaking under [the] load of pride and pretense. There is no release from our burden apart from the meekness of Christ."[10] He had in mind the wonderful (and eternal) invitation of Jesus: "Come to Me, all who are weary and heavy-laden, and I will give you rest. Take My yoke upon you and learn from Me, for I am gentle and humble in heart, and you will find rest for your souls" (Matthew 11:28–29 NASB). That promise of Christ builds on the beatitude that forms the centerpiece of this chapter.

"Blessed are the meek, for they will inherit the earth" (Matthew 5:5).

Inherit the earth? Jesus may have said it, but few of us believe it. The earth does not belong to the gentle and meek. A little life experience quickly tells us that the meek get taken advantage of. The gentle get run over by the powerful and beaten down by the assertive. The humble lose in the cutthroat competition of our culture. They all suffer at the hands of the violent and the aggressive.

Blessed are the meek. It seems ludicrous to suggest. *Meekness* is synonymous with *weakness* in the eyes of the world. Humility is what you accept when you

The burden of pride and pretense steadily crushes us.

have nothing to be proud of. But Tozer nails it on the head. The burden of pride and pretense steadily crushes us. It slowly suffocates us. Like minute doses of arsenic, it gradually poisons us and eventually kills us.

Meekness, then, is not a label for the weak but an antidote for the dying. Humility is not a trait of those with nothing to be proud of, but a deliberate choice by those who refuse to let pride steal their soul. Yet pride and pretense continue to slip in the side door.

John Stott, a leading Episcopalian priest and scholar in England, has written,

> I myself am quite happy to recite the General Confession in church and call myself a "miserable sinner." It causes me no great problem. I can take it in my stride. But let somebody else come up to me after church and call me a miserable sinner and I want to punch him on the nose! In other words, I am not prepared to allow other people to think or speak of me what I have just acknowledged before God that I am. There is a basic hypocrisy here; there always is when meekness is absent.[11]

Our sensitivity to what others think or say about us betrays the talon grip of pride in our lives. The ease with which a casual or careless word can wound us and stir us to sleepless nights exposes our pride even further. And our insistence that all is well when all is not well reveals the deep pretentiousness of our hearts.

Someone has printed a T-shirt with a picture of a cow on it. The cow lies on its back, with all four legs sticking straight up in the air—evidently stone dead. And the caption beneath it reads simply, "Everything's just fine!"

We want family, friends, neighbors, and co-workers to admire us. So we carefully shape an image and then defend it with vigor. Fearful that folk might see the real us (with our weaknesses and warts), we work tirelessly to project a preferred (and prideful) "false self," perhaps seeking to impress others by dressing well, driving expensive cars, and spending lavishly. David Benner writes, "Our false self is built on an inordinate attachment to an image of our self that we think makes us special."[12] And living this way, with one eye over our shoulder, shrivels the soul.

We need not characterize the meek as awkward, bumbling milksops without a backbone. True meekness often emanates from remarkable strength and courage. But more important, by embracing the meekness of Christ we begin to release the burden of pride and pretense. Once we reach the point where we care nothing for what others say or think of us because we only care for what Christ thinks of us, the burden lifts entirely.

Does this mean we adopt a reckless, cavalier, or condescending attitude toward others and their perceptions? Not at all. We love them deeply and listen to them sincerely. But we'll find rest for our souls not in perpetuating our pride and pretense but by embracing the meekness of Christ. And while this meekness ultimately leads to rest, it initially produces a great deal of upheaval.

Meekness cannot coexist with our self-admiration, self-determination, or self-promotion.

Meekness diminishes us at first. It cannot coexist with our self-admiration, self-determination, or self-promotion. It demands that we relinquish all of the "self" sins. Then, and only then, can it liberate us, although the process of refinement—letting go of everything that our culture has so long applauded—can feel very emptying.

My friend Scott emailed me. He and his wife were preparing to finish pastoring a congregation and felt unsure about their ministry direction thereafter. They had just been to a retreat center for pastors and their wives, when he wrote:

> I have had to face the drivenness of my own soul, and am in the process of repentance and, by God's grace, transformation. The

scary part is that I have been driven for so long, it has been my identity for so long, that once God burns it up, who am I? What is left? A stick of wood is transformed in the fire, but smoke and ashes are nothing. As I enter the fire of God's presence there is nothing left except Christ formed within me. These things He has communicated to me: I am His child, a servant, and a witness, and perhaps a manager in His house. My need to plant a hundred churches, save the world, and be Christ's hero . . . is burned up. Now I am waiting for Him to show me where to roll up my sleeves and be His child, a servant, a witness, and if He wills, a manager in His house. . . . In my good days I have faith in Him. In my not so good days, I hear the clock ticking and know that soon I will not have an income.[13]

Meekness comes with self-emptying, and while grounded in our trust of God's sovereignty and goodness, it can still produce great uncertainty at first. As Scott noted, it seems to produce nothing but smoke and ashes. We'd like the Lord to note our willingness to be meek and then bypass the actual "burning" of our ambitions and dreams. Couldn't He just honor them if we promised not to be too proud? But the One who creates *ex nihilo* ("out of nothing") somehow believes that smoke and ashes are even more than He needs to achieve His purposes in our lives and through our lives.

BLESSED . . . AND PROMISED

The meek are already blessed because the world does not control their hearts or drive their actions. Their confidence in the leading, provision, and protection of the Father makes them courageous in the face of hardship. Their trust in the Father's goodness makes them content amid turbulence. What could be more desirable?

From an external vantage point, meekness, which resists personal ambition and competition, appears soft. In reality, it reflects an unassailable strength within us. Meekness, which works hard but is never self-aggrandizing, seems destined to play second fiddle. In reality, it elevates us to a realm of faith and peace that the world craves but cannot achieve.

Many of the meek are also blessed for another key reason. While the aggressive and hostile elements of the world marshal against the meek, the meek refuse to join that fray. And their commitment to a lifestyle that neither complains nor quickly criticizes draws them into deeper and more meaningful relationships. The world hungers insatiably for such connection.

In this sense, the meek have already inherited the earth. They live lives that the world cannot diminish or crush. In another sense, the meek *will* inherit the earth because their hearts are so prepared and so practiced in walking with the Father.

Are we among the meek?

"You're blessed when you're content with just who you are—no more, no less. That's the moment you find yourselves proud owners of everything that can't be bought" (Matthew 5:5 THE MESSAGE).

SUMMARY STATEMENT

Meekness flows from a deep and unflagging confidence in the sovereignty of God and therefore does not need to assert itself. Yet for its quiet ways it exudes a peculiar and attractive strength. It avoids self-promotion and resists pride and pretense. And while the world wants to tread all over it, meekness proves as unstoppable as the tide. It shall prevail, and inherit the earth.

Discussion Questions

1. How do you feel about this definition of meekness: a commitment to non-self-assertiveness or self-interest, grounded in a deep faith in the sovereignty of God? What strikes you as helpful? What raises questions for you?

2. What steps can we take to deepen our faith in the sovereignty and goodness of God?

3. What stops biblical meekness from becoming a passive, complacent way of life?

4. What steps will you need to take to grow in the grace of meekness this week?

CHAPTER 4

Blessed Are Those Who Hunger and Thirst for Righteousness

"Blessed are those who hunger and thirst for righteousness, for they will be filled."

Mike hungered and thirsted for God, even before he came to know Christ. At twenty-two years of age, he quite literally renounced all things of the world in order to bring God out of His hiding place. He shared part of his story with me in an email:

> I showed God that I was serious by giving away everything I owned, except the clothes on my back. I didn't even keep my shoes. I changed my diet to organic and macrobiotic. I figured that if I was going to show God that I was serious enough for Him to listen to, that I would need to do everything the right way, or at least as right as possible.
>
> So at twenty-two years old, 5' 7", I weighed eighty pounds. I was a skeleton with skin on it. My renunciation had taken my life. By the time I realized how far I had gone, I was beyond human help.

I pleaded with God to help me get to a lake. I was in Hollywood, California, and I did not want to drop dead on the sidewalk.

I was so pathetic-looking as a hitchhiker that no one would pick me up. So after three days of trying to get a ride out of Hollywood, I headed back to my room. I remember crying on the way because I didn't think I could make it through another day.

All I had left, in my mind, was to make it to a lake. This was going to be the final showdown. I was going to find a secluded spot, lie down, and wait for God to prove to me that there was a reason to live. If He didn't, then I would choose to just lie there until I died.

But on the way home, a young man handed me a piece of paper. He began to tell me about Jesus. Something amazingly supernatural happened at that time. I felt a powerful force come down over me and let me know that I should listen to what this boy was saying.

I was not a Christian.

When he invited me to church, all I was concerned about was that it was on the way to Lake Isabella, and they would give me a ride. So I went. I sat through the services, glad that they had also offered me to spend the night there. I intended to head out for the lake the next day.

That night another young man gave the message. Providentially, he preached from Matthew 11:28: "Come unto me all you that are heavy laden, and I will give you rest." I stepped forward and gave my life to the Lord, and that night God delivered me from my "food trip" and began the process of healing my abused body (a process that took many years).

But the drive to attract God's attention and earn His favor remained with me every day—even after that decision. I never felt that I was doing enough, unless I was doing everything. I would lie down at night, after a long and hard day of witnessing on Hollywood Boulevard, and wonder if I had done enough to please the Lord.

It took me thirty years to discover that God really loved me, even though I didn't do everything.[1]

Few of us have been as hungry to find God as Mike was. He had an intense hunger and thirst to do "the right thing" in order to experience God, if God could be experienced at all.

In the first century, the Pharisees had this hunger to "do the right thing." Their fervor to please God and attract God's favor drove many of them to great lengths. They devoted themselves to keeping the Law fastidiously. On one occasion, a rich young Pharisee came to Jesus and asked what he must do to obtain eternal life. Jesus said, "Keep the commandments," to which the young man replied, "*All these things I have kept*; what am I still lacking?" (Matthew 19:17, 20 NASB). On another occasion, Jesus noted that the Pharisees were so meticulous about their religious duty that they tithed even the common garden herbs they grew—mint, dill, and cummin (Matthew 23:23).

According to Josephus, about six thousand of these Pharisees lived in Palestine in the first century.[2] And nobody did "the right thing" more than they. If God would reveal himself to anyone, they would surely be the first in line. Nobody deserved it more. Nobody could hold a candle to them.

A DISTURBING THOUGHT

Almost as soon as Jesus finishes uttering the Beatitudes at the start of His Sermon on the Mount, He delivers one of the most disturbing statements in the entire discourse: "Unless your righteousness *surpasses* that of the scribes and Pharisees, you will not enter the kingdom of heaven" (Matthew 5:20 NASB).

We might almost hear the gasp from the listeners. The Pharisees in the crowd probably just nodded in smug agreement. But everyone else must have been horrified, especially if this "righteousness" meant living more holy lives than these professional religious folk. We might draw our breath too.

On the face of it, what hope is there for any of us? Who could possibly be more meticulous about keeping the Law? More rigorous in their observance of the biblical statutes? More devoted to the religious customs and traditions than the scribes and Pharisees? No one. They represented the pinnacle of righteousness in the minds of many—and perhaps also in their own minds.[3] They did more things "right" than anyone else. If we have to exceed their efforts, we're not likely to succeed. It seems that Jesus dashes all hope for any of us.

But as with much of the teaching of Jesus, we tend to hear His words from one perspective only and feel utterly overwhelmed by it. Sometimes, however, He uses hyperbole—exaggeration—to make a point.[4] And at other times, He says something so startling that it demands a deeper look.[5] He says what He means and means what He says, but that meaning is not the superficial one that we might at first think. Such is the case here in His statement about righteousness.

Mike's story, which opened this chapter, is unusual at one level and common at another. How many of us have felt that the way to please God is to do the right thing? We beat up on ourselves over our failure to read the Bible enough, or our failure to evangelize everyone around us, or our failure to pray as much as we should, or any number of other spiritual shortcomings. We may not be shoeless in Hollywood, but we live with the nagging feeling that we're not doing enough to catch God's attention or earn His favor. And we can live like this for decades, or even a lifetime.

How in the world can our righteousness exceed that of the scribes and Pharisees?

A COVENANT WALK

Righteousness is not primarily about living right but about fulfilling covenant expectations.

Many of the hearers in that hillside crowd gathered around Jesus would have understood that righteousness (*dikaiosune*) is not primarily about living right but about fulfilling covenant expectations.

In the Old Testament, when two parties established a covenant, each party had certain responsibilities. For example, the ancient patriarch Jacob and his uncle Laban made a covenant together.[6] Laban promised not to pass a certain place to harm Jacob, and Jacob promised not to mistreat Laban's daughters or take any other wives apart from the two daughters. If Jacob kept his promise, he was "righteous." If he broke his promise, he was "unrighteous."

Early in the Old Testament, righteousness did not mean that someone lived a decent life or demonstrated high moral fiber. It did not indicate that a person made good ethical choices or always did the right thing. Instead, it referred simply and solely to whether or not a person kept the terms of the covenant. If they did, they were considered righteous.

Thus in Genesis 15:6 (NASB), we read that Abram "believed in the LORD; and He reckoned it to him as *righteousness*."[7] To the extent that Abraham trusted God ("believed in the LORD"), he fulfilled the basic covenant requirement asked by the Lord. He had trusted the Lord when He told him to leave his country, and relatives, and family home in Haran. Abraham had packed up and left "even though he did not know where he was going" (Hebrews 11:8). That kind of obedience and trust meant that Abraham was fulfilling his side of the covenant and was therefore righteous.[8]

When we understand righteousness in this way, the beatitude takes on a whole new meaning. Those who hunger and thirst for righteousness have an insatiable appetite to be in covenant with the Lord.

Furthermore, our righteousness exceeds that of the scribes and Pharisees because it depends not on our outer works but on our simple faith—the primary condition for entering into covenant with God.[9] If we trust Him with our lives, He calls us His children. It's as simple as that. Righteousness, then, is not about doing the right thing *for God*, but being right *with God*. Our righteousness exceeds that of the Pharisees when we accept the terms of the covenant that is greater than the covenant of the Pharisees.

INNER CHANGE

Dallas Willard suggests that *righteousness* also has another meaning: "true inner goodness."[10] While we typically want to define it in terms of right actions and right behavior, the early Greek philosophers like Socrates and Plato sometimes used the word to describe the desired state of the inner person.[11] Righteousness, then, can also refer to pure motives, a clean heart, a renewed soul, which then produce actions that bring healing and hope to those around us.

——◅❖▻——

Righteousness is not about doing the right thing for God, *but being right* with God.

——◅❖▻——

According to this definition, to hunger and thirst for righteousness could also refer to an earnest desire for transformation of our inner person. We long for the Father to restore us to His original design and intention. Our behavior and actions will, of course, also change, but we yearn for an inner renewal, not just an external modification. This too guides us to a righteousness that exceeds that of the Pharisees.

It's easy to settle for less. We'd like to throw aside our bad habits that keep causing us grief—addictions, explosive outbursts, harsh words, and all the rest. But biblically, to hunger and thirst for righteousness means that (a) we pursue a covenant walk with God by trusting Him, and (b) we focus on the heart (faith) rather than the hand (actions). We adopt the attitude of King David, who prayed, "Create in me a pure heart, O God, and renew a steadfast spirit within me" (Psalm 51:10).

"Blessed are those who hunger and thirst for righteousness, for they will be filled" (Matthew 5:6). As we've noted, this hunger and thirst for righteousness means we have a burning desire to know God. It's not that our actions are perfect, but our hearts are sincere in pursuing a walk with Him. Indeed, only hearts bursting with love for God would even lean in this direction.[12]

FIT TO BREAK

"Hearts that are 'fit to break' with love for the Godhead are those who have been in the Presence and have looked with opened eye upon the majesty of Deity."[13]

A. W. Tozer described nineteenth-century English poet and theologian Frederick Faber's love for Christ as "so intense that it threatened to consume him."[14] Many of us have felt such passion, so enamored (or infatuated) with someone that we can barely focus on anything else. We long to see him or her and hear their voice, utterly love-struck. Would anyone describe our passion for Christ that way? We may revere the Lord, respect Him, appreciate Him, and speak highly of Him. But does our love for Him threaten to consume us? This kind of hunger and thirst is always blessed.

We may teach about Him, evangelize for Him, build churches with Him, and pray to Him. But are our hearts "fit to break" as we think of Him?

The general coolness of Christendom, concerned with our own comfort, consolation, and convenience rather than consumed with Christ, suggests that many Christ followers—and we may be among them—have followed from too great a distance. Real passion is inflamed by proximity. The deepest affection is aroused by nearness. An all-absorbing love arises not from casual observation but intimate contact.

Many Christ followers have followed from too great a distance. Real passion is inflamed by proximity.

Of course, such love springs only from soft hearts; hearts warmed by grace, massaged by mercy, enrapt by redemption. As long as these transforming experiences remain no more than doctrines for discussion or principles for preaching, the coolness continues.

Our even-keeled, unexcited, controlled reflections on Him suggest we may have hearts that have yet to melt in His Presence. Our limited discussion *about* Him or *with* Him perhaps points to guarded hearts and restrained spirits.

Yet this tremendous truth remains: Whether or not our hearts have been enlivened by encounter and softened through surrender, His heart is "fit to break" over each of us. All of us. All the time.

The desperate longing of the Father for us never changes. He gazes down the road, relentlessly searching for us, just as the father longed for the return of his prodigal son in Luke 15. Overwhelmed by love, He pursues us. He always has, and He always will.

Those who hunger and thirst for righteousness could perhaps be described as "the people of the breaking heart"—not broken by misery but bursting with love. Fit to break.

Writing in 1930, Frank Laubach, renowned missionary to the Philippines and founder of an international literacy movement that has touched over 100 million lives, wrote: "Clearly, clearly, my job here is . . . to live wrapped in God, trembling to His thoughts, burning to His passion. . . . That is the best gift you can give to your [people]." And later, "It is the preacher's business to look into the face of God until he aches with bliss."[15]

INCOMPLETE ABUNDANCE

Writing on this beatitude—"Blessed are those who hunger and thirst for righteousness, for they will be filled"—Cameron Lee suggests, "We must leave a place for incompleteness, hunger and longing in the Christian life."[16] Perhaps he's correct. At one level our hunger and thirst is satisfied immediately by the Presence of God. At a deeper level we know that we've barely scratched the surface with regard to the richness of His Presence.

While Jesus promised that we'd "have life, and have it abundantly" (John 10:10 NASB), it sure doesn't feel that way at times. Waves of fear and anxiety still wash over us unexpectedly. Our tongues still speak criticism and poison before we can catch ourselves. Sickness and injury continue to plague us and distress us. Violence surrounds us and—worse—springs from us. Anger explodes. Wounds reopen. Pain persists. Even as we follow Jesus.

Our hunger and thirst are not fully satisfied. We are never as close to the Father as we'd like to be, and we discover that our desire for complete inner transformation is a lifetime process that never reaches completion.

"This side of heaven, the Christian life is characterized by unfulfilled longing, a spiritual groaning for things that will be but have not yet come to pass. All of creation groans together, waiting for God to finish the work he began in Jesus."[17] But couldn't it be different? What of health, wealth, and happiness? What about joy, peace, and abundance? What about power, success, and influence?

We naturally desire wholeness for our brokenness, healing for our sickness, abundance for our poverty, and peace for our conflict. But we dare not distort the gospel into a vehicle for escapism. Christ did not die on the cross to place us in a bubble. He did not endure humiliation to spare us the same. Instead, the suffering of Jesus—experienced in every life since Calvary—makes possible our eternal resurrection.

Our hunger and thirst is finally satisfied on the day of Christ Jesus when sin is defeated and death is conquered once for all. The psalmist cried out repeatedly, "How long, O Lord?"[18] and we still hear the same answer, "For now, but not forever." Meanwhile, His grace and His Presence respond to our groaning and grant us strength for adversity and hope for eternity.

THE WAY OF RENUNCIATION

A. W. Tozer concluded: "If we would indeed know God in growing intimacy we must go this way of renunciation."[19] Most of us don't want to know Him that badly. To renounce is to give up our own agenda and our own need for control. Affirmation sounds far more appealing than renunciation. We'd like easy change and settle for cheap intimacy. In short, we have a faint appetite, not a serious hunger or thirst.

It's not that we feel rebellious or cynical. Many of us want a deeper walk with Him—but at minimal cost, please. We'd like a large dollop of God on the side. Who wants a plate of just Him? Everything else takes center stage, at His expense.

We dare not distort the gospel into a vehicle for escapism.

We hold firmly onto our ambition. We insist on our habits and hobbies. We pursue pleasure and security, irresistibly attracted to our dreams, consumed by a passion to achieve and a drive to succeed.

Conversely, we provide safe harbor for our hurts, fears, anger, lust, and envy despite the raw wounds they inflict on us. And much as we'd like to be free of them, we feed them by refusing to renounce them.

Calvin Miller writes incisively,

> Never has there been a time when the wealthy evangelical church in America more certainly needs to hear her Savior saying, "If anyone would come after me, he must deny himself and take up his cross daily and follow me" (Luke 9:23).
>
> But we are wealthy, and our purses are so heavy that we cannot carry both our goods and his cross. So we cling to our wallets and leave the cross-bearing to those who have less to surrender. We would like to find some way to achieve godliness without repudiating our wealth.
>
> Our battle seems set against nature itself. Our appetites are so much a part of us![20]

The good, the bad, and the very ugly all rule in our hearts because we fail to pursue the Father with intensity . . . and renunciation. We may have a mild appetite for Him but not a ravenous hunger. Yet ironically, contentment in life comes only from craving, not complacency.

Even as a pastor, I found myself at times more devoted to

pursuing the church than pursuing God. I satisfied myself with doing the work of the Kingdom rather than walking with the King. My "calling" subtly became self-serving. At times, all I had renounced was the way of renunciation.

We may have a mild appetite for Him but not a ravenous hunger.

God created us to enjoy Him first, and any deviation from that biblical truth—that creation purpose—ultimately yields little more than futility and frustration. Yet we persist in our pursuit of "the other." Tozer observes: "God's gifts now take the place of God, and the whole course of nature is upset by the monstrous substitution."[21]

Will we walk the way of renunciation?

Our reservations are understandable. Renunciation sounds like a descent into passivity, aimlessness, and nothingness. But biblical renunciation never leaves a void. Jesus invites us to take up our cross and follow Him. It's a breathless step to take, and requires more courage than most of us can muster. But deep, rich, and authentic intimacy with God requires His exclusive access to the throne of our hearts.

What have we grown to love more than Him? Will we bravely walk the way of renunciation? Our answer is integral to the blessing that Jesus wants to pour out upon our lives.

Blessed . . . and Promised

Dr. D. Martyn Lloyd-Jones, who preached for thirty years in Westminster Chapel in London, wrote:

We are not meant to hunger and thirst after blessedness; we are not to hunger and thirst after happiness. But that is what most people are doing. We put happiness and blessedness as the one thing that we desire, and thus we always miss it; it always eludes us. According to the Scriptures, happiness is never something that should be sought directly; it is always something that results from seeking something else.[22]

The fourth beatitude calls us to righteousness: a covenant walk with the Father, and inner transformation. Those who desire this above all else experience blessing both now and in the future. In the present moment, we find that as we draw near to Him He draws near to us (James 4:8). And, in the midst of the "unfulfilled," we discover that His grace is sufficient for us.[23] Finally, when we rest in the Presence of Christ for eternity, the hunger and thirst we have now will be fully satisfied.

"You're blessed when you've worked up a good appetite for God. He's food and drink in the best meal you'll ever eat" (Matthew 5:6 THE MESSAGE).

SUMMARY STATEMENT

When Jesus blesses those who seek righteousness, He does not refer to people who live perfectly moral and irreproachable lives. He calls out those who hunger to know God and desire inner personal change more than anything else. These people have hearts bursting with love for God and they're willing to renounce their own agenda. They shall be satisfied.

Discussion Questions

1. How does the concept of *righteousness* as "maintaining covenant with God" and "yielding to inner transformation" change your perception of the term?

2. In light of this chapter, rate your hunger and thirst for righteousness on a scale of 1–10. What steps might you take to move that up one notch this week?

3. Is it possible to nurture a heart "fit to break" (bursting) with love for Christ? If so, how?

4. What is your response to "the way of renunciation"?

CHAPTER 5

Blessed Are the Merciful

————— ❧ —————

"Blessed are the merciful,
for they will be shown mercy."

We did not treat him kindly at all.

I attended high school in Sydney, Australia. My class included a Jewish boy named Emmanuel, and in that all-boys school he stood out. He came from an Orthodox Jewish family and wore a kippah on his head at various times. During the Jewish Feast of Tabernacles, Emmanuel ate his lunches in a hut on the back of a flatbed truck driven onto campus. This observed the Jewish custom of eating meals in a tent or hut to commemorate their wilderness wanderings.

Emmanuel also attended Saturday Hebrew School, where he learned Jewish traditions, Hebrew language, and Scripture—as if Monday to Friday at Sydney Boys' High School was not enough. He studied voraciously; he always had his head in a book.

While most of us boys were kicking a tennis ball around in a lunchtime game of makeshift soccer, Emmanuel studied. While we practiced cricket down in the nets, Emmanuel studied. While we played rugby (and took beatings in the interschool competitions), Emmanuel studied and excelled. And we resented it.

He made an easy target for us, and we regularly teased, taunted, harassed, and hurt him with our words. We told ourselves and each other that we only intended to "bring him down to our level." After all, his achievements made us look ordinary, and we all felt the pressure to perform well academically. But our words—mean, hurtful, belittling, sarcastic, demeaning—functioned as curses in his life.

In Australia, high school spans six years (grades 7–12) and during that time I watched the changes in Emmanuel. He took up running, perhaps because it afforded him time in solitude. And since he could eventually outrun most of us, he received a modicum of respect for it. In the classroom, his behavior shifted from pure attentiveness to an element of disruptiveness. He worked to fit in with the crowd, to be accepted by his peers—to stop the curses. In a sense, our negativity changed him negatively. The curses bore fruit—at least for a time.

When the opportunity arises for us to fire a fair shot at someone it takes a special grace to stand down. It takes mercy.

Emmanuel's story is not unique. It happens over and over every day in hundreds of thousands of school yards, homes, and workplaces. In ungodly moments, people use their words to wound each other. Bullies taunt, parents yell, and supervisors intimidate. Many times these negative words come from a cruel spirit that enjoys wielding power. But we're all prone to use harsh words, words spoken in anger and judgment—perhaps even anger and judgment that are justified. And when the opportunity arises for us to fire a fair shot at someone, it takes a special grace to stand down. It takes mercy.

78

The fifth beatitude that Jesus proclaims was not easy to hear in the first century and is no easier to hear today. "Blessed are the merciful, for they shall receive mercy" (Matthew 5:7 NASB).

DEFINING MERCY

The root term for *mercy* (*eleos*) that Jesus uses in Matthew 5:7 has various connotations and produces a degree of confusion for us.

Some folk liken mercy to simple kindness.[1] But kindness is a trait that two friends may express to each other—favors for one another, small thoughtful acts done in the course of everyday life: an ice cream cone, a cleaned room, flowers, a meal. None of this is mercy. Mercy is far more than an act of kindness between two friends or two equals.

Others compare mercy with compassion, but compassion frequently describes a feeling we have for those who suffer. When we see young children caught in war zones or disaster areas, we feel compassion—a longing to help in some way. And while mercy has an element of compassion, the two are not the same. Mercy is far more than the feeling or act of compassion.

As a young boy I regularly wrestled with my dad. Those times rank among the fond memories of my childhood, though my father would usually end up applying his feared "Indian death lock" that had me calling for mercy. In the United States, the term *uncle* serves the same purpose. This use of the word *mercy* begins to approach the biblical idea, but only slightly. Mercy is what someone in a stronger position extends to someone in a weaker position.

The *Merriam-Webster Dictionary* defines mercy in this way: "Compassion or forbearance shown especially *to an offender or to one subject to one's power.*"[2]

Mercy is what the Roman Emperor extended when two gladiators, one poised to slay the other, looked to him for a decision and he gave the thumbs-up, sparing the life of both men for another day.

Some of the most famous lines from William Shakespeare's play

The Merchant of Venice speak to this view of mercy. In the Venetian courtroom, Portia tries to convince the moneylender Shylock to dismiss his charge against Antonio. Portia argues that mercy is a divine attribute, and we best reflect God when we exercise it.

> The quality of mercy is not strained.
> It drops as the gentle rain from heaven
> Upon the place beneath. It is twice blessed;
> It blesses him that gives, and him that takes.
> It is mightiest in the mightiest; it honors
> The crowned monarch better than his crown.
> His scepter shows the force of temporal power,
> Which invokes awe and majesty,
> And wherein sits the dread and fear of kings;
> But mercy is above this sceptered sway;
> It is enthroned in the hearts of kings;
> It is an attribute to God himself;
> And earthly power then looks most like God's
> When mercy seasons justice.[3]

BIBLICAL MERCY

Biblically, mercy is when we forgo an opportunity to take vengeance, punish, or humiliate someone. We show mercy when we relent from anger and forgive someone rather than extract a justified pound of flesh from them. It is merciful to forgive a debt rather than sue for it. It is merciful to pay back evil with good (Romans 12:21). Indeed, forgiveness stands at the very center of mercy, and this virtue of mercy resurfaces regularly throughout Scripture.

Mercy is when we forgo an opportunity to take vengeance, punish, or humiliate someone.

When the Lord instructed Israel to build a tabernacle for their wilderness wanderings after they left Egypt, He also had them construct the ark—the box that would signify His Presence among them. The lid of that box served a special purpose. It was known as "the mercy seat" (Exodus 25:17–21) to remind Israel that God is merciful. Each year the High Priest would sprinkle the blood of a sacrifice on the mercy seat so that the Lord might relent of His judgment and show mercy (see Leviticus 16:14–15). Mercy is what the Lord showed when He turned from His burning anger (Deuteronomy 13:17; Psalm 6:1). Later, the apostle Paul declares that the Lord shows mercy to us despite our disobedience (Romans 11:30–31).

In Matthew's gospel, mercy is what two blind men cried out for as they followed Jesus (Matthew 9:27). Mercy is what a Canaanite woman begged of Jesus on behalf of her demon-possessed daughter (Matthew 15:22). Mercy is what an unnamed father asked of Jesus as he grieved his son's dangerous fits of epilepsy (Matthew 17:15). In each instance, helpless individuals who did not deserve favor pleaded for the Son of God to show them favor. But they had more than simple favor on their minds.

The Jews believed that illness and affliction were signs of God's judgment for sin.[4] To beg for mercy was to ask for that judgment to be lifted. The blind men were not looking for mere sympathy. They wanted forgiveness, and then the healing that would come with it.

Interestingly, Matthew records for us one of Jesus' stories that none of the other gospel writers preserve, and it provides a helpful clarification of mercy:

> The kingdom of God is like a king who decided to square accounts with his servants. As he got under way, one servant was brought before him who had run up a debt of a hundred thousand dollars. He couldn't pay up, so the king ordered the man, along with his wife, children, and goods, to be auctioned off at the slave market.
>
> The poor wretch threw himself at the king's feet and begged, "Give me a chance and I'll pay it all back." Touched by his plea, the king let him off, erasing the debt.
>
> The servant was no sooner out of the room when he came upon

one of his fellow servants who owed him ten dollars. He seized him by the throat and demanded, "Pay up. Now!"

The poor wretch threw himself down and begged, "Give me a chance and I'll pay it all back." But he wouldn't do it. He had him arrested and put in jail until the debt was paid. When the other servants saw this going on, they were outraged and brought a detailed report to the king.

The king summoned the man and said, "You evil servant! I forgave your entire debt when you begged me for mercy. *Shouldn't you be compelled to be merciful to your fellow servant who asked for mercy?*" The king was furious and put the screws to the man until he paid back his entire debt. And that's exactly what my Father in heaven is going to do to each one of you who doesn't forgive unconditionally anyone who asks for mercy. (Matthew 18:23–35 THE MESSAGE)

This mercy, then, expresses an act of restraint and forgiveness extended by the stronger to the weaker; extended by one who has received mercy to one who needs mercy. James understood that our tendency is to be harsh with each other despite any forgiveness we may have received. So he wrote: "Judgment without mercy will be shown to anyone who has not been merciful. Mercy triumphs over judgment!" (James 2:13).

> *In a culture obsessed with personal rights and retribution, mercy has long since lost its way.*

In a culture obsessed with personal rights and retribution, mercy has long since lost its way. Anger and judgment flow unrestrained. And the fruit of this anger and judgment is always additional pain and division between us.

MERCY WITHOUT RESTRAINT

We cannot give what we have not first received, and herein lies the irony of the fifth beatitude. We don't show mercy to get mercy.

Quite the contrary. We can only truly extend mercy when we have already received it. Then, in a self-regenerating cycle, we give what we have received, and we receive more.

The Reverend Richard Wurmbrand, a Romanian evangelical pastor who worked in the underground churches of Romania during the Communist era of the mid-twentieth century, spent fourteen years in Romanian jails and labor camps because of his Christian faith. He relates a moving story from one of his times in prison.

Wurmbrand shared a cell with a Romanian-Orthodox deacon named John Stanescu, among others. The Communists were holding both men in a slave labor camp when someone informed Colonel Albon, the director of the camp, that a prisoner had preached about Christ. Colonel Albon went into the cell demanding to know the perpetrator. When no one responded, his anger boiled over and he threatened to flog everyone. Still nobody stepped forward. So he started at one end of the cell and systematically beat each man. When he came to Stanescu, he was infuriated that the man had not stripped off his shirt to receive the caning.

Stanescu looked directly at Albon and said, "There is a God in heaven, and He will judge you." His defiance surely meant that he'd be beaten to death. But suddenly a guard called the colonel urgently to the main office because some Communist generals had arrived unexpectedly. On his way out, Albon said to Stanescu, "We will see each other again soon."

To everyone's surprise, the generals arrested the colonel, and after an hour Albon was indeed back in the cell—as a prisoner. When the guards tossed him in among the other prisoners, many of the inmates jumped to lynch the former labor camp director. It would surely have been a death sentence, except that John Stanescu defended his former enemy, receiving many blows himself as he protected the tormentor from the enraged prisoners.

In Richard Wurmbrand's words, "Stanescu was a real priest. Later I asked him, 'Where did you get the power to do this?' He replied, 'I live Jesus ardently. I always have Him before my eyes. I also see Him in my enemy. It is Jesus who keeps [my enemy] from doing even worse things.' "[5]

Could *we* show such mercy? Could we step in to protect our enemy when we finally had the power to crush him?

Very few of us will likely spend time imprisoned or beaten with canes because of our faith. But mercy is needed in many spheres of life. How often do we repay evil with evil, especially evil words for evil words?

Do we harbor grudges and brood with resentment? *Blessed are the merciful.* Do we plot ways to get even with those who have hurt us? *Blessed are the merciful.* Do we tear down those who have unjustly hurt us? *Blessed are the merciful.*

Beyond the Beatitudes, this theme of mercy weaves through the rest of the Sermon on the Mount. When a brother has something against us, we're to show mercy by taking the initiative, going to him, and seeking to be reconciled (see Matthew 5:23–24). We are not to retaliate against those who are evil toward us, though we may feel quite justified to do so (Matthew 5:39). We are to love and pray for those who call themselves our enemies[6] (Matthew 5:44). We are to forgive others their transgressions against us, or our Father will not forgive *our* transgressions (Matthew 6:15).

How difficult this must have been for the first hearers. Their very survival seemed to be at stake. The Romans had taken everything they valued and set up a political system to oppress and exploit them. And Jesus says, "Blessed are the merciful." Just when the people feel primed for open revolt, ready to fight their oppressors, Jesus praises those who restrain their anger and their judgment.

Blessed is the heart that refuses to call anyone an enemy.

It may be no easier for us. Loving our enemies is not easy. But blessed is the heart that refuses to call anyone an enemy and that resists anger and judgment.[7]

On the cross, Jesus expressed mercy to his executioners: "Father, forgive them, for they do not know what they are doing" (Luke 23:34). He gave His life mediating the Father's mercy, bringing good news to the broken and the weary, and extending grace and mercy to those who were hostile. Thus the apostle Paul could later say that through Christ, the Father has "canceled out the certificate of debt consisting of decrees against us, which was hostile to us; and He has taken it out of the way, having nailed it to the cross" (Colossians 2:14 NASB).

A SEVERE MERCY

Sheldon Vanauken and his wife, Davy, shared a special and intense love for each other. Indeed, as a symbol of their love, they named their dream schooner the *Grey Goose*, because the grey goose mates for life, and if its mate is killed, it flies on alone and never takes another. The two studied at Oxford and developed a friendship with C. S. Lewis. They even became followers of Christ. But gradually Sheldon realized that he was no longer Davy's primary love—God was. And a quiet jealousy brewed within him.

Not long after, Davy succumbed to a fatal illness. Sheldon felt shattered, bereft, and broken. In the midst of his anguish he resolved to learn all that he could from this heartrending experience of grief. In his book *A Severe Mercy*, he chronicles the journey as he came to understand the meaning of "a mercy as severe as death, a severity as merciful as love."[8]

Sheldon concluded that Davy's death had several results: "It brought me as nothing else could do to know and end my jealousy of God. It saved her faith from assault. . . . And it saved our love from perishing."[9]

God's jealousy has often provoked Him to anger with His people. The nation of Israel felt this anger and judgment constantly throughout their history as they rejected and neglected the Lord. And the Lord, rather than destroy the nation (which He felt sorely tempted to do at times),[10] relented and showed a severe mercy by sending them instead into exile, a place from which He had every intention of restoring them.

We might hope that the mercy of God is never so severe with us, but His mercy always has an ultimate end, to lift us to a better place. Lack of compassion, lack of grace, lack of mercy would leave us to wallow in grief and self-pity. But in the midst of severity, the Father comes to us, wraps His arms around us, and carries us. In the moment of crisis, the loving Father restrains His judgment and delivers us, preserves us, and guides us into a new abundance of life. He shows mercy time and again, and His mercy does not mean inaction. It leads Him to very specific engagement in our lives, to redeem us.

BLESSED . . . AND PROMISED

As a high schooler in the 1970s, I stood by and watched the teasing and taunting of Emmanuel. For nearly thirty years I had no contact with him, though I often wondered what had become of him. Then, surprisingly, through a series of events, we reconnected. I apologized for the hurtfulness we had inflicted those many years ago—the caustic and cruel words—wondering how he might feel about that chapter of our lives. He might readily have harbored bitterness and anger, but instead he expressed mercy. He had moved on, he said, refusing to allow unforgiveness, resentment, anger, or bitterness to take root. And his mercy freed us both. He had been free for a long time. I had not.

"Blessed are the merciful . . ."

". . . for they shall receive mercy." Yes, as we show mercy toward each other, we also receive it from each other. We reap what we sow. And we receive it also from the Father. Our forgiveness of others, made possible only by the transforming power of Christ within us, bears testimony that God himself has forgiven and will forgive us.

"You're blessed when you care. At the moment of being 'care-full,' you find yourselves cared for" (Matthew 5:7 THE MESSAGE).

SUMMARY STATEMENT

Merciful people show restraint and forbearance when they might easily (and even rightfully) display anger and judgment. They express grace rather than revenge, and trust God to take up their cause. Grudges and resentment find no root in their hearts, and they are blessed because they live free of bitterness. They receive mercy because they sow it in the lives of others.

Discussion Questions

1. How does this chapter's definition of mercy align with (or alter) the way you have always thought of mercy?

2. What do you think about the suggestion that mercy ought to be a defining feature of our faith?

3. Why is it a blessed act to be merciful? What does it say about our hearts? And how does it shape our lives?

4. Is there anyone in your life who has somehow hurt you and for whom you need to restrain your anger and offer forgiveness? How will you do this?

CHAPTER 6

Blessed Are the Pure in Heart

"Blessed are the pure in heart,
for they will see God."

On February 1, 1960, four black college freshmen walked into a Greensboro, North Carolina, dime store. That Monday afternoon they bought a few small items and then did the unimaginable. They sat down at the "whites only" lunch counter and ordered coffee. Their actions sparked a tide of civil rights protests that changed America.

Franklin McCain, Joseph McNeil, Ezell Blair Jr., and David Richmond sat near an older white woman on the silver-backed stools at the F. W. Woolworth store. Their actions were carefully premeditated; they told their families the day before what they intended to do, aware that this sit-in could result in violence against them.

They had no way of knowing how the sit-in would end, but they were tired, they were angry, and they were ready to change the world. So on that Monday afternoon, the four men stayed at the lunch counter until closing, waiting to get service. The next day, they came back with fifteen other students. On the third day, three hundred joined in. By the end of the week, one thousand sit-in demonstrators had joined their cause.

Little did they imagine that their action would motivate sit-ins across the country. Indeed, within two months, thousands of people had joined sit-ins in fifty-four cities in nine states—and within six months, the Greensboro Woolworth lunch counter was desegregated. Over the next five years, the demonstrations helped pass the 1964 Civil Rights Act and the 1965 Voting Rights Act.

Franklin McCain, one of the original four students, recalled that the older white woman who sat just a few stools down from them watched them very carefully that fateful first afternoon. Then, when she had finished her donut and coffee, she stood and walked over to the young men. She stepped behind McNeil and McCain, put her hands on their shoulders, and with a very calm voice said, "Boys, I am so proud of you. I only regret that you didn't do this ten years ago. Good luck!" And with that she walked out the front door. [1]

Those words of blessing gave added courage to the four young men. The woman surprised them with her support, and her words fortified them and fueled the fire in their souls. Her blessing helped significantly, but the single-minded focus of those four young men made all the difference. They had no doubt about what they wanted to see happen.

And so we come to Jesus' sixth beatitude: "Blessed are the pure in heart, for they will see God."

PURE IN HEART

Commentators and Bible translators have long struggled to interpret the phrase *pure in heart* with any clarity. The New Century Version puts it this way: "They are blessed whose thoughts are pure." But who has pure thoughts? The human heart is so filled with mixed motives, jealousy, fear, envy, greed, and selfishness that it's hard to imagine anyone having truly pure thoughts. Perhaps Jesus should have said, "Blessed are those who have fairly pure thoughts." Then at least a few folk might squeak in the door—a very few.

Did Jesus really intend to speak an unattainable blessing?

Young's Literal Translation of the Bible expresses the beatitude with these words: "Happy the clean in heart." But the idea of a clean heart proves as elusive and murky as pure thoughts.

Dallas Willard shows a creative flair when he writes: "Blessed are the pure in heart—for whom nothing is good enough, not even themselves; perfectionists—a pain to everyone, themselves most of all—who never feel worthy."[2] Willard correctly assumes that Jesus had real people in mind when He spoke this blessing.

Eugene Peterson also gives the beatitude some practical meaning and moves us toward the truest sense of it when he writes, "You're blessed when you get your inside world—your mind and heart—put right" (THE MESSAGE). Perhaps Jesus is not speaking so much about perfection as alignment. Could a pure heart be one that is "put right"?

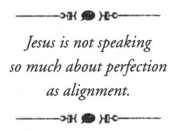

Jesus is not speaking so much about perfection as alignment.

The most helpful way for us to consider purity of heart is to see it as single-minded focus—a focus as intense as four young black college students in 1960.

In 1846, thirty-three-year-old Danish philosopher Søren Kierkegaard penned the first of his classic "Edifying Addresses," titled *Purity of Heart Is to Will One Thing.* Kierkegaard challenged his readers, in part, to examine their lives and the influence that the crowd has on us in producing duplicity, insincerity, inauthenticity, and disharmony. To paraphrase him: "To will only one thing, genuinely to will the Good, as someone who is aware of eternity and their own responsibility before God, to want nothing more than to hold fast to God, which all of us can do—this is what unites us together in the purest way."[3]

Kierkegaard's understanding of purity of heart—single-minded attention, intense focus—drills to the core of the phrase. Surely Jesus looked at those around Him and saw at least some people who were deeply dedicated to seeing God. And He pronounced such people "blessed."

J. B. Phillips got it right when he translated "pure in heart" as "utterly sincere." Blessed are those whose lives keep looking sincerely toward God, for they shall see Him.

OUR GAZE

A. W. Tozer wrote:

> One hundred pianos all tuned to the same fork are automatically tuned to each other. . . . So one hundred worshipers [meeting] together, each one looking away to Christ, are in heart nearer to each other than they could possibly be were they to become "unity" conscious and turn their eyes away from God to strive for closer fellowship. Social religion is perfected when private religion is purified.[4]

The key to harmony and unity lies not in our efforts to "get along" but in our alignment with Christ. As Kierkegaard noted, when we look upon our circumstances or ourselves rather than Him, we inevitably devolve into division, battling over opinions and preferences, feeling hurt and victimized.

Conflict and dissension have marred the church since its beginning. The church in ancient Corinth experienced prejudice, pride, and false piety, which threatened to tear it apart. And churches today, large and small, struggle with the same sins.

Many of us feel deeply disillusioned by the politics of the local congregation and suspect that the solution to our pain is to align ourselves with new or smaller gatherings, where we might avoid the dynamics of "the institution." We naïvely believe that smaller, less-structured, more relational groups can avoid the pitfalls of conflict that have wounded us in the past. Yet we overlook that even marriage itself (the smallest and most intimate of communities) is not immune to conflict.

Tozer defined faith as "the gaze of a soul upon a saving God."[5] And he rightly reminds us that until we are all tuned to the same fork, we cannot be anything but discordant.

The purity of heart honored by Jesus in the sixth beatitude is best understood in these terms: not as moral purity but as a correct gaze—"Let us fix our eyes on Jesus" (Hebrews 12:2). Renowned fifteenth-century monk Thomas à Kempis understood the blessing of this fixed focus. He wrote: "Oh, when will this blessed and desired hour come when you will fill me with your presence and be all in all to me? As long as this is not given to me, my joy will not be complete."[6]

To the extent that we look around more than up, we'll breed an environment for disruption. If we focus more on others than on the Savior, we'll experience discouragement. Our hope for the unity of the church—and the unity of our families and marriages—lies not in articulate visions but in believers who devote themselves to set "the gaze of a soul upon a saving God."

Herein lies the essence of being pure in heart.

CURLED FINGERS

Michelangelo's famous sixteenth-century frescos on the ceiling of the Sistine Chapel in Rome include that memorable scene of two hands almost touching. The one hand—from the figure slightly lower than the other—has a relaxed wrist and slightly curled fingers while the higher figure reaches out quite decisively with the forefinger, seeking to make contact.

To seize the hand of God means to hold nothing else.

The latter is the hand of God, always extended. The former hand belongs to us, casually indifferent and wondering whether to touch or withdraw.

The image may surprise us. Humanity, just a little lower than God himself, lacks enthusiasm to connect with Him. Meanwhile, the Father extends himself as we ponder our level of interest.

Will we open our hand?

The image portrays us altogether too accurately. We extend our arm in the Father's general direction, vaguely and distractedly aware of His Presence, but remain reserved and a little closed. And for good reason.

We intuitively know that to seize the hand of God means to hold nothing else. To grasp Him demands a complete and utter focus on Him. But we want so much else—autonomy, control, power—so we curl our fingers slightly, or even tightly. Our hearts are distracted and divided, not pure.

Jesus defined eternal life as knowing the Father and the Son (John 17:3)—the intimate knowledge that comes through contact, not proximity. Thus Michelangelo's fresco expresses not only his strong artistic capacity, but a fundamental challenge to our timidity and halfheartedness. It calls us to purity of heart.

The ordinariness of much of our Christian experience arises not from the Father's aloofness but our hesitation, our curled fingers.

The ordinariness of much of our Christian experience arises not from the Father's aloofness but our hesitation, our curled fingers.

Will we grow more open-handed, ready to reciprocate the Father's reach and release our reservations? Only as we fix our gaze on Him and reach out boldly and sincerely toward Him can we truly see Him and know Him. Our apathy and indecision blind us to His glory.

However, the blessing for the pure in heart assumes not just focused attention but faithfulness.

STRANGE FAITHFULNESS

The apostle Paul opened his letter to the Ephesians with this simple address: "To the saints . . . *who are faithful* in Christ Jesus" (Ephesians 1:1 NASB).

We admire faithfulness and marvel when a couple remains married for a lifetime. Few of us expect it.

There were 2,162,000 marriages in the United States in 2008.[7] Of these, about 1,000,000 are likely to end in divorce based on current statistics.

We're heartbroken but not horrified by part-time or short-lived faithfulness. And spiritual faithfulness seems no more certain.

On the one hand, some abandon the faith altogether. On the other, many redirect their faithfulness. They model tremendous faithfulness to Scripture, to the church, to leadership, to programs, to other believers . . . but are short on faithfulness to Christ.

They'll cry foul, and claim that their devotion to these other things proves their devotion to Christ. But it rings hollow. It sounds strangely like the husband who exclaims, "I've been working these long hours for *you!*" or "You know these people need me!"

Excuses. Excuses. Excuses.

Faithfulness to the person is supplanted by busyness or personal preferences.

The bride too often looks past the bridegroom. It's a strange faithfulness. Yet when the apostle Paul opens his letter to the Ephesians, he honors them, above all, for their faithfulness to Christ Jesus. It's not steadfastness in doctrine that he first commends, nor diligence in outreach, nor devotion to the church. It is faithfulness because of a person and to a person: Jesus.

Perhaps we should ask, "Are we 'in Christ' or merely 'near Christ'?" Are we attached to Christ or merely attracted to Christ? Do we speak to Him or about Him? Do we practice the Presence of Jesus or simply extol His ideals? It's the difference between purity of heart—or not.

We must not define the essence of Christianity by rites and rituals or doctrines and dogmas, but by a key relationship. Jesus, the risen Lord, is not an ancient icon, but our current companion. Our faithfulness to Him and walk with Him transcend *everything*.

"To the saints . . . who are faithful in Christ Jesus." The pure in heart may not be perfect in every thought or motive, but they are faithful and committed.

SEEING MORE

Purity of heart, then, denotes the heart with an intense focus, a fixed gaze, an attentive reach, and a deep faithfulness. It also speaks of the heart that sees farther and beyond—the heart that believes in and strives for the eternal promises of the Father.

It's easy to see that the strong survive, the quick make the profits, and the educated get power. School-yard bullies and corporate bullies play the same game, but on different fields. The violence, abuse, greed, sickness, and corruption all around us are frightening. And rightly so, when they're all we see.

Christ followers sometimes drop their line of sight to the chaos around them rather than the calling beyond them.

Even biblically literate Christ followers sometimes drop their line of sight to the chaos around them rather than the calling beyond them.

The apostle Paul's first prayer for the Ephesian believers remains pertinent and powerful for each of us today . . . that our hearts may be enlightened to know the hope of our calling, the riches of our inheritance, and the tremendous power of God for us who believe. (See Ephesians 1:18–19.)

But we too easily miss the thrust of the passage.

We have confidence in the future, an inheritance that comes after our death, and God's power to raise us from the dead. It's not the common message of immediate fame, fortune, prosperity, and health.

As we grapple with job losses, home foreclosures, debt collectors, troubled children, deaths of loved ones, the shame of past decisions, raw wounds inflicted by others, and so much more, we can easily descend into darkness. Harsh circumstances seem to highlight our weakness and insignificance and can plunge us into despair.

A little "enlightenment" could go a long way. In fact, the journey of faith *must* take us beyond weekend worship and casual fellowship. To survive and thrive amid the brokenness we experience will demand more than gritty determination.

We need fresh vision. We need to see more.

Don't misinterpret Paul's prayer as fatalism—a passive acceptance of life's hardship and grim endurance until it's finally over. Not at all! Enlightened hearts (pure hearts) set us free right now—free to act courageously, free to forgive, and free to endure disaster without despair. Enlightened hearts (pure hearts), gripped with hope, confident in blessing, and dead certain of resurrection, transcend the chaos.

They see more. Therefore, they live more. And they are blessed here and now.

Holy, Hungry, and Humble

In the fall of 2009, some students of mine completed more than one hundred fifty interviews with leaders across the United States—CEOs, business owners, managers, military personnel, entrepreneurs, civic leaders, politicians, and pastors. The interviews sought to identify common key leadership principles, consistent with Scripture. The responses were fascinating and instructive, but none more so than one senior church leader who distilled his insights into a single statement.

"Be holy, hungry, and humble."

Those three terms drive to the foundations of Christian discipleship and present a challenge in a culture far more drawn to sin, selfishness, and celebrity status. They also reflect core elements of the pure heart.

Holy. The pursuit of purity and the commitment to live set apart for Christ sound good but fade in the face of contemporary values and the pressure to fit in. We'd like just a moderate dose of holiness, thanks, but end up with little more than an inoculation. Yet the Lord continues to declare, "Be holy, for I am holy" (1 Peter 1:16 NASB).

Hungry. Do we live with an insatiable appetite to know Christ and draw close to God? (Philippians 3:8). Or do we find ourselves driven by other impulses: the hunger of personal ambition, recognition, or success? Do we long for the Lord as much as we might for a marriage partner, or a child, or a better job? What gnaws at us most and deepest in this season of our lives?

> *Do we long for the Lord as much as we might for a marriage partner, or a child, or a better job?*

Humble. In lives filled with pride and pretense, humility confronts us. We like recognition, credit, and appreciation. It feels good when people notice us. So we hang out shingles that display our achievements and accolades, beginning with our preschool graduation certificate. But the fruit of this pride never ripens to something sweet (1 John 2:16–17).

"Holy, hungry, and humble" describes the essence of Christian discipleship, not just Christian leadership. This triumvirate of terms perhaps captures the heart of what it means to be a Christ follower, and captures the essence of what it means to be pure of heart. They represent more than three nicely alliterated words. They denote lives on a collision course with our culture and a transformational journey with Christ.

Holy, hungry, and humble is the way of Christ. And as we embrace the Way, we grow increasingly mindful of the battle for our hearts that rages all around us. Blessed are the pure in heart, if they're able to withstand both the violent and the subtle onslaughts against their hearts.

Of course, we face any number of challenges and distractions to "pure hearts." The culture around us aims to numb and inoculate our hearts against the pure focus we most desire.

INOCULATED HEARTS

Cameron Lee, in his book *Unexpected Blessing*, writes a couple of paragraphs that jolt us back into consciousness.

> [Our] video-saturated entertainment culture has changed the very way we think. For example, not only does the television news over-expose us to human folly night after night, the very way in which the news is presented lulls us into indifference. We see our favorite local news team, immaculately groomed, serving up a smorgasbord of unrelated snippets of stories. First, a story about political genocide; if the anchor is shocked by it, it doesn't show in her face. The story is read with a certain detachment. Our knowledge of the world is being mediated by someone who presents each tragedy as just one more piece of information. And even if we are inclined to reflect more seriously on the story about political genocide, before we know it, we find ourselves looking at a graph showing how many points the Dow Jones average fell today or watching a commercial about laundry detergent. This is news as entertainment, a program that even has its own theme song.
>
> News as entertainment puts us at a distance from the tragedies represented in the stories told. We are given enough to stimulate our voyeuristic impulses, but not enough to make us feel grief or remorse about what happened. As James Twitchell has observed, the cardinal rule in television is to never make the viewer feel bad.[8]

Web-based news is no different. Scroll over the headline and get the 12- to 15-word summary: "200,000 estimated dead in Port-au-Prince"; "2 U.S. killed by bomb in Afghanistan"; "Wall Street ends week with a steep slide"; "Actress Jean Simmons dies at 80"; "Caught on tape: amazing dog rescue." And after a quick scan, we shift to the next task, untouched and unstirred by the more grim realities of the world. We find that our hearts, desiring to focus purely on Christ, are no longer able to focus on anything of significance at all.

Does our thirty-minute news grab help or hurt us? Are our news-junkie tendencies inoculating our hearts against the compassionate heart of Christ? Are we so desensitized by the dispassionate presentations of tragedy that we simply accept them rather than respond to them?

In the struggle for our hearts, is CBS, CNN, NBC, or Fox News winning the battle on a battleground we've not identified? Our purity of heart, our devoted attention to Him, and our insatiable desire to see Him come under fire every day. Of course, the solution is not simply to quit watching the news (although a lot less news would probably be a good thing). Rather, this serves as an example of the fragmentation and inoculation of our hearts that happens in multiple ways every day.

It takes great discipline and courage to increasingly align our hearts with the Father's heart.

BLESSED . . . AND PROMISED

In studying the impact of Franklin McCain, Joseph McNeil, Ezell Blair Jr., and David Richmond following their sit-in at the F. W. Woolworth store in 1960, Bill Chafe, a Duke University historian, has concluded, "Greensboro was the pivot that turned the history of America around [in the struggle of African-Americans for freedom]."[9] Their focused, premeditated, nonviolent, and courageous defiance provided a catalyst for national change.

Jesus declared, "Blessed are the pure in heart." And they are indeed blessed. Those with a burning passion and focused drive typically produce change and achieve results. But more important, in the context of the Sermon on the Mount, those who are utterly sincere in their pursuit of God will see Him. We can have no greater desire. And the blessing and promise of Christ to each of us is that the Father does not hide from those who seek Him, nor resist those who desire Him. To the contrary: He reveals himself and draws close. What a blessing.

"You're blessed when you get your inside world—your mind and heart—put right. Then you can see God in the outside world" (Matthew 5:8 THE MESSAGE).

SUMMARY STATEMENT

"Pure in heart" describes those with a single focus and desire—for God. Such people yearn to know Christ and they reach out to Him without reservation. They demonstrate faithfulness to Him and live with unflagging faith in the eternal promises of the Father. We might describe their lives as holy, hungry, and humble. And they shall see God.

Discussion Questions

1. How do you feel about Kierkegaard's statement/definition— "Purity of heart is to will one thing"?

2. How can we better fix our gaze on Christ?

3. What would it mean for you to open your hand more to the Lord and look to Him with less reluctance?

4. Why is faithfulness such a key element of a pure heart? And how can we grow in it?

CHAPTER 7

Blessed Are the Peacemakers

"Blessed are the peacemakers,
for they will be called sons of God."

Elizabeth DiNunzio dreamed of being a high school Spanish teacher, and in a couple of weeks she would graduate from two-hundred-year-old Mount Saint Mary's University in Emmitsburg, Maryland. She was also excited about her first 26.2-miler, the Pittsburgh Marathon, just five days away. So on April 28, 2009, the twenty-two-year-old slipped on her pink running top and black shorts and headed out for a run. It would be good to get in a few last miles before the race.

Elizabeth chose a route that took her down a two-lane country road popular with joggers and past the home of the university president, Dr. Thomas Powell, about half a mile from the campus. Dr. Powell was about to pull out of his property to return to campus. He saw Elizabeth to his left and a red Nissan pickup truck approaching from his right. Next, he heard a loud thud as the pickup hit DiNunzio.

Moments later [Powell] spotted one of DiNunzio's shoes on the grass across the street, and then, about 10 feet ahead on the lawn, DiNunzio. Powell threw his car in park, left the engine running, and sprinted to her while calling the university's public safety office on his cell phone. . . .

Powell cradled DiNunzio in his arms, her blood blanketing his clothes and hers, her pulse growing fainter. "You are loved," he told her before she died. "You are loved."[1]

The scene horrifies us. How would most of us respond in such a crisis? We'd surely call 9-1-1 too. But in the panic of the moment, how many of us would have the presence of mind—or conviction—to utter a blessing? Yet Thomas Powell spoke words of blessing, not to save Elizabeth in the moment but to prepare her for eternity—words that reflected a reality greater and stronger and more enduring than the very accident she had just suffered. His words, simple and brief, spoke a truth to her to give her peace and prepare her for the very Presence of God.

Peacemakers often find themselves in the line of fire.

"Blessed are the peacemakers," said Jesus. But peacemakers seek to impart blessings, not receive them. And in the midst of the pain and conflict that abounds in our world, peacemakers often find themselves in the line of fire, in the midst of violence, chaos, and mess.

Garrison Keillor, in his book *We Are Still Married*, asks, "What else will do except faith in such a cynical, corrupt time? When the country goes temporarily to the dogs, cats must learn to be circumspect, walk on fences, sleep in trees, and have faith that all this woofing is not the last word."[2]

Peacemakers must indeed have faith, but they don't "learn to be circumspect, walk on fences, and sleep in trees." They engage the world around them. They don't just wait out the woofing. They get down in the yard with the dogs and help find solutions to the conflict. And that's no easy vocation. Peace may be an honorable pursuit in a world of war, violence, and suffering, but it's also hazardous. Many peacemakers have ended up as victims themselves.

Jesus was crucified by an angry mob on the basis of false testimony and dirty politics. Mahatma Gandhi survived at least five assassination attempts in the last fifteen years of his life, until he finally fell to a point-blank bullet on January 30, 1948. John Dear, a renowned Jesuit priest and peace activist of our day, has been in and out of jail repeatedly over the years for his nonviolent civil disobedience in the cause of peace.[3] And so many tens of thousands of unnamed peacemakers have been imprisoned and even died standing up for their ideals.

A NONVIOLENT PATH

In August 1963, on the steps of the Lincoln Memorial in Washington, D.C., Martin Luther King Jr. addressed a crowd of 250,000 people—white and black—and urged them to pursue peace without violence.

> There is something that I must say to my people. . . . In the process of gaining our rightful place we must not be guilty of wrongful deeds. Let us not seek to satisfy our thirst for freedom by drinking from the cup of bitterness and hatred. We must ever conduct our struggle on the high plane of dignity and discipline. We must not allow our creative protest to degenerate into physical violence. Again and again we must rise to the majestic heights of meeting physical force with soul force.[4]

Less than five years later—April 4, 1968—Martin Luther King Jr. would be struck down by a sniper's bullet as he stood on a motel balcony in Memphis, Tennessee. Peacemakers don't always enjoy the fruit of their endeavors. The violence they denounce has a way of turning upon them in a world overrun with anger, fear, and hostility.

—————⊰⊱—————

Peacemakers do not consider the possibility of their death to be adequate grounds for quiet acquiescence to violence.

—————⊰⊱—————

Jesus did not say that peacemakers would experience peace, but that they would be called sons of God.[5] Inasmuch as they follow the example of the One who refused to call down legions of angels to protect himself, peacemakers become like Christ. They are sons of God because they grasp the futility of violence and do not consider the possibility of their death to be adequate grounds for quiet acquiescence to violence. Peacemakers understand deeply that the ends never easily justify the means. The process is as important as the outcome. Peace achieved through intimidation is no peace at all. Calm attained through threats cannot last.

Anyone who has ever thought that peacemaking is for the weak or timid has failed to grapple with the extraordinary strength of character that authentic, consistent peacemaking demands. In fact, those who resort quickly to violence demonstrate the blind herd mentality of our culture. Such people, duped to think that the path to peace winds through destruction and aggression, fear to confront the flow of the culture around them.

Charles Carl Roberts IV, heavily armed and with evil intent, stormed and barricaded a small Amish schoolhouse in Nickel Mines, Pennsylvania, on October 2, 2006. Before the ordeal ended, five young schoolgirls lay dead in that schoolhouse, as did the gunman. The senseless carnage shocked the entire pacifist Amish community.

Under the best of circumstances, grief can cloud our judgment and drive us to actions we may later regret. But in a stunning and national headlines–grabbing act, elders from that Amish community went to the widow of the shooter *on the very night of the schoolhouse attack* and extended grace and forgiveness to her and her children.[6] That woman and her children were victims too, and the Amish elders refused to let one man's violence breed aggression and division within their community. Mrs. Roberts was a murderer's wife, but she was also a grieving widow. Labels can help—and harm.

NO MORE LABELS

In Ephesians 2, the apostle Paul writes about the peacemaking work of Christ: "He Himself is our peace" (2:14), and he notes all the labels that Christ's peacemaking abolished: "Gentiles . . . 'Uncircumcision' . . . separate . . . excluded . . . strangers . . . no hope . . . without God . . . far off" (Ephesians 2:11–13 NASB).

Labels are helpful on canned goods but generally harmful on us. Yet long before calories, ingredients, and FDA approvals showed up on our grocery items, we had been assigning labels to each other.

Many negative labels stick like glue throughout our lives. And even if they're not constantly re-spoken by others, we regularly repeat them within our own hearts.

My *Random House College Dictionary* separates the word *label* from the word *libel* with twenty-three pages of other words, but in life the two words often belong side-by-side. Which of us has not been wounded by a label? Who among us has not been scarred by a painful sticker?

In Max Lucado's delightful children's story *You Are Special*, the wooden Wemmicks all live in a village together and take delight in giving each other stickers.

The pretty ones, those with smooth wood and fine paint, get stars. But if the wood is rough or the paint chipped, the Wemmicks give dots. The talented ones get stars too, but others, with no special skills, get only dots.

Punchinello, an unattractive, not-very-talented Wemmick, is covered with dots—and feels that he deserves them. That is, until he visits the woodcarver, Eli, who made all the Wemmicks and lives on the hill behind the village. From him, Punchinello realizes how special he is, and when he does, a dot falls to the ground. [7]

Some labels puff us up; most beat us down. War and racism rely on labels to dehumanize people and make it easier to vilify, hate, or even kill them. Labels produce a convenient distance.[8]

So we live in the world at arm's length.

The labels create an exclusion zone that allows us to disregard or even hurt others. Labels detract from the reality and humanity of those around us.

But the gospel won't let us live in such isolation. It demands that we treat others as people, not products. And peacemakers understand this first and foremost.

When we perpetuate destructive labels, we deny and defy the gospel, the good news that Christ breaks down all the barriers and restores us again to the Father and to each other. When we believe negative labels that others apply to us, we are allowing lies to keep us from entering the doors of freedom and intimacy with Christ.

Peacemakers have the conviction and courage to identify the painful labels that we speak to each other and then refute them.

When the apostle Paul wrote to the Ephesian Christians, he spelled out a number of wounding and distancing labels. Then he explained that the work of Christ brings us all into one body, fellow citizenship, and a single family (God's household). The label that defines us best is simply the *beloved children of God*. It opens the door to life at a new level.

Peacemakers have the conviction and courage to identify the painful labels that we speak to each other and then refute them. This separates them from peace-keepers, those who work diligently to maintain the status quo, not challenge it. A peacemaker calls sin what it is; a peace-keeper confronts no one and nothing. A peacemaker leads others to repentance and change; a peace-keeper tries to simply keep a lid on hostilities. A peacemaker decries intimidation; a peace-keeper may use it.

Blessed are the peacemakers, not because their task is easy or likely to be appreciated but because in the endeavor they reflect the ministry of Christ himself.

Homes and businesses, schools and communities need peacemakers more than ever, though peacemakers remain rare in our culture.

PEACEMAKERS

Violence confuses us: We both fear it and embrace it; it horrifies us and entertains us at the same time.

On the one hand, the thought of a violent home invasion scares the daylights out of us. We've all entertained fears of what Oklahoma resident Donna Jackson faced in reality. In December 2009 she was at home alone when a man tried to smash his way through her home's rear glass door. Armed with a shotgun, fifty-seven-year-old Jackson called 9-1-1 and begged for help. By the time police got there, Billy Riley, fifty-three, had been shot and killed.[9] The story itself can raise anxiety within some of us. It's our worst nightmare.

On the other hand, we spend hundreds of millions of dollars on entertainment systems and video games that turn violence into fun.[10] We hate the idea of a physical beating, but we'll watch people kick, punch, and beat each other in a ring—strangely thinking that the ring somehow justifies or sanitizes the brutality.

The bloodlust of our culture has never been higher. Listen to the violent language. Watch the violent images. Experience the aggression on the roads and the fierceness in the stadiums. In such an environment, peacemakers—or even peace-talkers—are *persona non grata.* Nobody likes them: "They're soft." "They're weak." "They're out of touch." Theodore Roosevelt's foreign policy of "speak softly but carry a big stick" has become a common personal mantra. We're willing to talk for a short while but always ready to fight when provoked.

Everyone knows that peacemaking is for fools and idealists.

Everyone except Jesus.

When Jesus honored and blessed peacemakers with His seventh beatitude, He called all of His followers to turn peacemaking into a life pursuit.

The challenge, of course, is simply this: Can we be peacemakers while we share the passion for violence that pervades our culture?

The Son of God came without violence into a violent world. He confronted the established order not with swords and weapons but with words. He came not with bloodlust but a willingness for limited bloodshed—just His own.

Can we be peacemakers while we share the passion for violence that pervades our culture?

Contrary to some distorted views, Jesus' cleansing of the temple (see John 2:13–16) does not justify everything from berating abortionists to shooting Islamists.

The ancient prophet Isaiah described the promised Christ as "Mighty God, Everlasting Father, *Prince of Peace*" (Isaiah 9:6). And those who follow Him must surely take this title with utmost seriousness. To the extent that we participate in the violence of our culture, we diminish our capacity—and perhaps our desire—to make peace. Aggressive language, hostile actions, and a heart that views violence for entertainment do not nurture a peacemaker.

THE COST OF PEACEMAKING

As we've already noted, peacemaking is not the easy route. Most people who embrace this as a consistent way of life find that it demands more than they ever expected.

John Woolman was one of the early American settlers back in the eighteenth century, before the Revolutionary War. He was also a Quaker, who took peacemaking seriously. Most people who know his name today associate him with the earliest movement to abolish slavery in America—a century before Abraham Lincoln and the American Civil War of 1861–1865.

Woolman, a gifted businessman and entrepreneur, limited his business activities so that he could travel among the Friends (as Quakers were known) and urge those who owned slaves *not* to bequeath them to their children in their estates but to free them, and to always treat them with dignity and honor. This "peacemaking"—interceding on behalf of slaves for their good treatment and release—came at considerable cost to Woolman. We could measure the cost financially, because it required that he curtail his business endeavors and therefore limit his financial prosperity. Woolman's convictions also demanded considerable time away from home; he spent weeks and months traveling with this message. In addition, his mission produced stress and heartache, as reflected in his journal.

But peacemaking was a life value for Woolman and extended well beyond his advocacy for slaves. When it became clear that the king's representatives were raising taxes from the colonies to wage war against the French, Woolman and others concluded that they could not pay those taxes. In a letter signed by a number of prominent Friends of the day—landowners and men of influence—we read:

> Being painfully apprehensive that the large sum granted by the late Act of Assembly for the king's use is principally intended for purposes inconsistent with our peaceable testimony, we therefore think that as we cannot be concerned in wars and fightings, so neither ought we to contribute thereto by paying the tax directed by the said Act, *though suffering be the consequence of our refusal, which we hope to be enabled to bear with patience* [italics added].[11]

This decision came to be known as "scrupling the payment," and those who scrupled the tax did suffer considerably for their decision. Woolman wrote that "distress was made on their goods" by the collectors and constables, but they endured the hardship because it was such a matter of conscience. The decision, of course, was far from popular with their neighbors, who feared a possible invasion. And not all Friends agreed with the radical step. Nor did Woolman find this an easy conclusion to reach. He wrote in his journal: "It requires great self-denial and resignation of ourselves to God to attain that state wherein we can freely cease from fighting when wrongfully invaded, if by our fighting there were a probability of overcoming the invaders."[12]

Woolman and others understood the call to peacemaking. They took it most seriously and paid dearly to be peacemakers with integrity. Would we show such diligence, fortitude, consistency, and conviction as peacemakers?

"Blessed are the peacemakers, for they will be called sons of God."

RELEASING RESENTMENT

Most of us struggle to be peacemakers when we have been hurt or wounded. It's one thing to promote peace in the world, or to decide to embrace nonviolence as the Kingdom way. But when we pay a personal high price for an injury of some sort, peacemaking takes on new proportions.

On December 17, 2009, James Bain, a fifty-four-year-old Florida man, used a cell phone for the first time, calling his mother to tell her that he would be home for Christmas.[13] After thirty-five years behind bars, Bain was released by Judge James Yancey based on fresh DNA evidence that Bain could not possibly have been guilty of the crime for which he had spent his entire adult life in prison. This innocent man had lived in jail since 1974, when he was just nineteen years old.

As Bain left the courtroom a free man, reporters had a list of questions they wanted to ask. Among them, someone asked, "Do you harbor any anger or resentment?"

James Bain had missed out on every opportunity that most Americans enjoy—the opportunity to further his education, to date, to marry, to have children, to establish a career, to attend church, to enjoy family celebrations, and so much more. All of that had been stripped away from him when he was tossed in jail on no more evidence than an inaccurate identification by one person. A boatload of resentment would be entirely understandable.

But James Bain answered simply and clearly, "No, I'm not angry—because I've got God."

To be a peacemaker requires that we release our own resentment and bitterness. Many of us allow hurt and injustice to build up within us. We feel aggrieved and then grow increasingly attached to our outrage. Not James Bain. He learned long ago that bitterness bites only the one who shelters it. And the answer to our umbrage is Christ. The better we know Him and the closer we walk with Him, the more His peace guards our hearts and minds and we extend peace to those around us. Forgiveness and reconciliation begin within us before they can extend from us.

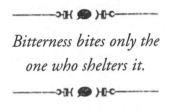

Bitterness bites only the one who shelters it.

PEACEMAKING EVERY DAY

We ought not to think of peacemaking as something that only statesmen or rare individuals can do. As followers of Jesus, we all share the mission to be peacemakers. And the task of peacemaking is perhaps most frequently required in the smallest ways and the most obscure settings.

Christ calls us to serve as peacemakers in our marriages. When conflict suddenly blows up, will we fuel the fire or quench it? With our children, will we teach them to defend their territory or make peace? In the workplace, do we contribute to the gossip and the division or serve to ameliorate it? In the church, do we maintain the unity of the Spirit or stoke disunity?

We err if we believe that peacemaking requires a major offense. Every time we see hurt and woundedness in those around us, will we seek to serve them or steer clear of them? Of course, our task is not to solve everyone's problems or get involved in everyone's disputes, but there will be times when Christ calls us to step in; not simply to sympathize with the conflicted but to steer them toward peace.

In a distorted and confused world, peacemakers find opportunities in every corner. But our best peacemaking emerges from our own practices and experiences of peace. As we learn to respond with grace toward irritating neighbors and unfriendly co-workers, we also grow equipped to help others do the same.

BLESSED . . . AND PROMISED

When Dr. Thomas Powell held Elizabeth DiNunzio and blessed her in those final moments of her life, he functioned as a peacemaker—seeking to bring peace to her on the threshold of eternity. And irrespective of the impact upon her as her life ebbed away, his words of peace shaped him in that moment too. Peacemakers are indeed blessed, because as they refuse to accept violence, division, and hostility between people, they share in the very heart of God himself. Those who pursue peace *with* all men and *between* all men best capture the essence of God's mission in the world. "God, who reconciled us to himself through Christ and gave us the ministry of reconciliation . . . has committed to us the message of reconciliation. We are therefore Christ's ambassadors" (2 Corinthians 5:18–20).

"You're blessed when you can show people how to cooperate instead of compete or fight. That's when you discover who you really are, and your place in God's family" (Matthew 5:9 THE MESSAGE).

SUMMARY STATEMENT

Peacemakers oppose the way of violence, though they often become victims of it. And Jesus calls them "sons of God"—a reference to kings and rulers in the Old Testament. Peacemakers oppose the hurtful and divisive labels that we often apply to each other and frequently pay a

high price for their convictions and efforts, without resentment . . .
but with blessing.

Discussion Questions

1. How would you define the differences between peace-
   keepers and peacemakers?

2. Describe some of the labels that breed conflict in marriages,
   families, school yards, and communities.

3. What steps could you take as a peacemaker?

4. Identify some of the signs that we live in a culture of violence. Why is it important to stand against this culture?
   How can you prevent being drawn into it?

5. What did you find most challenging or helpful in this chapter? Discuss.

CHAPTER 8

Blessed Are Those Who Are Persecuted Because of Righteousness

"Blessed are those who are persecuted because of righteousness, for theirs is the kingdom of heaven."

Father Tom Hagan moved to Port-au-Prince, Haiti, in 1997 and began a ministry in Cité Soleil, the city's largest and most miserable slum. He oversaw the construction of eight schools that educated 9,000 children (the only free schools in the country), a free clinic that cared for 20,000 people, homes that sheltered 150 of the poorest of the poor, and projects for the elderly that served 800 individuals. The ministry also had a kitchen area that fed hot meals to over 10,000 people a day.

On January 12, 2010, Father Hagan and the executive director of the ministry, Doug Campbell, had just sat down to chat when a devastating earthquake struck the city. In the mayhem that followed, both men escaped serious injury when a young Haitian man quickly dragged them outdoors. Their building then, like so many others, collapsed.

Within a day or two it became apparent that the earthquake had destroyed absolutely everything that the ministry had constructed over the years.

On January 24, twelve days after the earthquake, Father Hagan sent an email to Tom Roberts, editor-at-large of the *National Catholic Reporter*. Hagan wrote:

> Everywhere you go, you will see the church reaching out now and helping the people. The Missionaries of Charity (Mother Teresa's nuns) are just amazing. The people here have a great faith. . . . What makes me most proud of my church is that the message we give the people is that they have enormous worth in the eyes of God and that they are infinitely loved and that this terrible disaster is in no way a punishment from God.
>
> I recently said this in a sermon and the people all stood up and began clapping and cheering. I had to ask the altar server why they were clapping (I thought that I had said something wrong because my Creole is not good) and he said, "Father, no one ever tells them that they have worth."[1]

"No one ever tells them that they have worth." Amid the chaos and carnage, many of the Haitian people of Cité Soleil looked to God. Put down, neglected, rejected, and despised, these suffering people of the slums found tremendous comfort in a word of affirmation and blessing. Yet again we see that we ought not underestimate the power of a spoken word to touch a heart when that word is personal and sincere.

Those who suffer find great comfort in a blessing. And as Jesus spoke to the hillside crowd, He saved His last beatitude—the eighth—for the persecuted and the afflicted, perhaps the largest group within that audience. "Blessed are those who are persecuted because of righteousness, for theirs is the kingdom of heaven."

BECAUSE OF RIGHTEOUSNESS

People suffer persecution for many reasons. The Nazis persecuted the Jews during World War II because they considered the Jews ethnically inferior. Black Americans understand the pain of persecution based on nothing more than skin color. A friend of mine fled Cambodia during the terror-filled reign of Pol Pot, after my friend's father was arrested and hauled away (never to return) for being an educator. Many women around the world experience persecution because of their gender. Schoolchildren have a way of isolating and persecuting those who simply fail to fit in. And slum landlords persecute and intimidate their poverty-stricken tenants so they can continue to extort from them.

Persecution is rife in our world. People like to exert their power over others everywhere we turn for a wide range of reasons. But behind all persecution lies one of two basic motives—a hunger for power or simple fear. The same was true in Jesus' day. The world has not changed.

Behind all persecution lies one of two basic motives—a hunger for power or simple fear.

Bullies, despots, and dictators use persecution to satisfy their insecurities, and no one poses a greater threat to them than those who do not—and will not—fear them.

In chapter 4, we saw that the term *righteousness* speaks to something larger than just doing the right thing. We noted that righteousness refers to keeping covenant terms and pursuing a heart change. It does not mean that we act perfectly in every situation. It means that we pursue God and open our hearts for His Spirit to transform our inner person. To such people—persecuted because of their godly pursuit—belongs the Kingdom of heaven.[2] And people who seriously pursue God and find their security in Him have the least to fear from other people, and therefore pose the greatest threat. Those who pursue righteousness in the biblical sense of the word have nothing to lose in this world, and therefore attract special attention from the thugs and antagonizers of this world.

SPIRITUAL BLESSINGS

Our covenant convictions and our confidence in the Father's blessings beyond this moment make all the difference. Indeed, only our faith in the spiritual blessings of the covenant will be enough to sustain us through physical hardships.

The apostle Paul knew this all too well, and he desperately wanted followers of Christ to grasp it. So he wrote to the Christians at Ephesus: "God . . . has blessed us *with every spiritual blessing* in the heavenly places in Christ" (Ephesians 1:3 NASB). Those spiritual blessings include the fact that God chose us (v. 4), "predestined us to be adopted as his sons" (v. 5), redeemed us (v. 7), and revealed the mystery of His will to us (v. 9).

In an old Frank & Ernest cartoon, Frank tells the parson, "I'm tired of blessings in disguise. If it's all the same to you, I want one I can recognize immediately."

We've probably all felt that way. When we lose a job or take a pay cut, we don't need spiritual blessings, we need financial answers. When the test results come back and we have a malignant growth, we don't want lofty spiritual thoughts, we want our health back. When we see our spouse at the end of each day and they're as cold as ice or as fiery as Tabasco sauce, we don't want theologizing; we'd be grateful for a flicker of peace and calm or tenderness.

Spiritual blessings, such as those Paul describes to the Ephesians, sound fascinating, but we generally want something practical, something to help our bank accounts, our bodies, or our relationships.

Of course, when the wheels get loose on our wagon, we might pursue spiritual blessings, but usually with the hope to convert them into material improvements. Yet the apostle Paul declares that the

Lord has blessed us with every spiritual blessing, and he considers them definitive and life-grounding. They matter more than any other blessing—more than food, shelter, health, or wealth.

Our constant focus on material blessings ("God has blessed me with a spouse and children and a home and a job and food and finances") betrays our inattention to the deeper, richer, and more sustaining spiritual blessings. And of course if we fail to live with a firm grasp of these spiritual blessings, then which of us would endure any persecution at all? Persecution will threaten all the material elements of our lives, and if those elements turn out to be our primary source of comfort and security, we'll protect them by doing whatever is necessary to avoid rather than endure persecution.

Herein lies one of the insidious dangers of the prosperity gospel. If we believe God wants us to have health and wealth in this life, we're likely to hold to them more tightly than we ought to. If we believe that our happiness is His greatest desire, then we won't endure persecution or suffering; we'll avoid it at all costs. In the end, the prosperity gospel breeds a soft and distracted version of Christianity that knows little of these spiritual blessings and even less about endurance and perseverance.[3]

> *If we believe that our happiness is His greatest desire, then we won't endure persecution or suffering.*

Our spiritual ups and downs will only subside when we finally embrace these spiritual blessings as the foundation for our lives—the fruit of our pursuit of the Father. These blessings include terms like *chosen, holy, blameless, adopted, redeemed, forgiven, graced,* and *loved,* which Paul uses in Ephesians 1:3–8. *Nothing* matters as much.

One of the great deficiencies in the walk of faith for many of us is our blindness to these spiritual blessings and our preoccupation with the approval of others or material well-being.[4] Yet "every spiritual blessing" belongs to us. That's what we need most, always. Those who face persecution can only face it with this faith. And such faith is blessed indeed.

GOSPEL WORTHY

In another of his letters, the apostle Paul urges Christ followers to live gospel-worthy lives, and no one needs to hear this more than those who face persecution.

Few people conduct their lives worthy of *anything* beyond themselves anymore.

We may act with civility, decency, and generosity to enhance our own reputation. It feels good when folk compliment or praise our good behavior. So we live in a manner worthy of people's praise. Thus, the vast majority of us conduct our lives much of the time with our own interests in mind.

The apostle Paul, however, calls us to an entirely different life focus and motivation. "Whatever happens, conduct yourselves in a manner *worthy of the gospel of Christ*" (Philippians 1:27).

We're tempted to let civility and decency do double duty. Nice people surely reflect a nice Jesus. But niceties don't cross Paul's mind. In the context of Philippians 1, he's thinking of service, sacrifice, and suffering.

To live worthy of the gospel of Christ is *not* to be sweet and friendly, *nor* to be kind and thoughtful—honorable though such actions may be. No. "Worthy of the gospel of Christ" means something else.

Part of our difficulty today lies in our murky definition of *the gospel*. Ask ten believers to define it and we're likely to hear ten different responses: promises of prosperity, assurances for eternity, assertions of forgiveness, invitations to the Kingdom, and more. And while Paul would not dismiss the significance of these, he would reduce the gospel to something we rarely discuss: resurrection.

The gospel of Christ is the guarantee that death produces life.

His resurrection and our promised resurrection render all threats null and void. Death has lost its power. Fear of the grave is no fear at all for followers of Jesus. Therefore, to live worthy of this good news is to demonstrate utter devotion to Christ, even in the face of apparent sacrifice and suffering.

The terms *sacrifice* and *suffering* generally intimidate us. We don't like inconvenience and discomfort, let alone sacrifice and suffering. But the gospel, fully understood, transforms these words. Sacrifice and suffering no longer denote loss and pain. We'll not fear them and speak of cost and hardship. Instead, we will speak of *privilege* and *honor* when we face hardship for the cause of Christ. Indeed, the blood of the martyrs is the seed of the Kingdom, and those who share in the sufferings of Christ will share in His eternal blessings too.

In a world that still marvels at sacrifice, it ought to be the norm among Christ followers. To live a life worthy of the gospel means far more than simply being honest, truthful, friendly, gentle, or thoughtful. It means, instead, that we die daily to ourselves, sacrifice what we have held to so dearly, and present ourselves as living and willing sacrifices on the altar before Christ (Romans 12:1–2). In the world's eyes, such behavior is radical, extreme, and a little unnerving. In the eyes of Christ, it is to live a life worthy of the gospel.

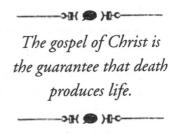

The gospel of Christ is the guarantee that death produces life.

Those who persevere through persecution do so not because they have stronger wills, greater pain thresholds, or less feeling, but because they understand gospel-worthy living and have an unshakable confidence in the gospel; that because of the cross, death's outcome is always resurrection. Thus, persecution is but a pathway to glory. Such people, with such faith, stand out among us as blessed. Theirs truly is, and will be, the Kingdom of heaven.

Stimulus—Choice—Response

Years ago I attended a seminar on team leadership put on by Rockhurst University. Dr. Dave Jensen was one of the presenters. He outlined a number of strategic skills for better management, but made one comment that stood out above the rest: "Between stimulus and response is a place called choice." He drove home a simple point. When conflict arises, we've got choices to make.

Two people may respond to the same circumstance very differently.

About that same time, I hired a woman to join my work team. Rosemary was Japanese-Brazilian by background. She spoke both Japanese and Portuguese fluently. English was her third language, and it wasn't her best, though I marvel that anyone can speak three languages!

We had an incident in which an online adjunct professor had been less than gracious with Rosemary. She wrote an email back to him, rather matter-of-fact but not rude at all, in responding to his demands. He took some exception, and Rosemary came to me for advice. I looked at her email and could see how a prideful professor might have his feathers ruffled a little. So I mentioned to Rosemary that perhaps next time in a similar circumstance she might touch base with me *first*.

How would she respond? How would *we* respond?

Some of us would grumble and grouse about pride and arrogance. We'd feel slighted and offended. We'd brood and justify ourselves. That would be normal—and acceptable—for most of us. Not for Rosemary. She came to me the next day just before lunch and asked me to read an email she had written to the professor. You can imagine my surprise. Rosemary had left work the evening before and headed straight to a bookstore, where she searched for a book on writing business letters. She found one that outlined how to write (in English) a good letter of apology, and then had spent time that night at home, and the next morning at work, composing a letter of sincere apology for having offended or hurt the professor in any way. When she had the final draft ready, Rosemary asked me to read it and give her my opinion.

Needless to say, I knew in that moment that I had hired an exceptional person. Her English would improve just fine with time, but I saw a gem that had lain hidden. I've rarely been as gracious, as self-effacing, as humble as Rosemary. Too often, I've had the typical responses to hurt and offense.

Dave Jensen had this to say: "People and circumstances don't bother us. It's our thoughts about those people or circumstances that bother us." He was absolutely correct. Otherwise, every circumstance (stimulus) would affect us all (response) the same way; and we know that is not the case. Between stimulus and response is a place called choice.

Jesus implicitly taught this. When he taught about forgiveness, He intended to short-circuit the incessant mulling that plagues some of us, a mulling that usually represents a choice to grow bitter. Similarly, the apostle Paul understood the value of setting our minds on things above (the spiritual blessings), not on the things that are on earth (Colossians 3:2). When we refuse to dwell on evil or hurt or disappointment, such things have little power in our lives. And that's a matter of choice.

Are you working with someone who drives you crazy? Your craziness is your choice. Are you angry because of how someone has treated you or because of circumstances that have changed for you? Your anger is your choice.

The old notion of cause and effect is not the same as the notion of stimulus and response. Cause and effect is fairly predictable and constant. If I let go of a ball, it will fall. And that will be true for everyone who drops a ball. Cause—effect. But stimulus and response are much more variable.

As men and women created in the image of God, we have the

capacity to make multiple conscious choices. It's unpopular to say this in our day when everyone is encouraged to view themselves as victims—of government, of corporate greed, of poor parenting, of bad schooling, of bullies, of bad bosses, of a biased legal system, and so on. The mentality of victimization downplays the matter of choice. It thus also diminishes responsibility. When I am the victim, I am not the responsible party. And that excuses my response. But this victim mentality produces far less than blessing in our lives. Its fruit is usually marked by resentment, bitterness, unforgiveness, retaliation, hostility, anger, and a dozen other destructive traits.

This is not to say that we don't suffer. The purpose of this chapter is to acknowledge that persecution and hardship and suffering happen, sometimes for righteousness' sake and sometimes not. But between stimulus and response is a place called choice.

> *A victim mentality produces far less than blessing in our lives.*

If we want to harbor bitterness, resentment, and grudges, we can do so. Society will sometimes even support it. But part of maturing into Christlikeness means recognizing that dire circumstances do not eliminate our capacity to choose. Thus Christ "for the joy set before him endured the cross" (Hebrews 12:2). And Paul, despite persecution and hardship for the cause of Christ, wrote that "we overwhelmingly conquer" because of the unstoppable love of God (Romans 8:37–39 NASB).

Perhaps we ought to exhort one another afresh that "between stimulus and response is a place called choice." If someone strikes us hard we may bruise (cause and effect), but if they wound us emotionally or relationally or professionally we will determine the significance of the blow. We decide the response. No one makes us angry or bitter or afraid. We make these choices. Stimulus—choice—response.

Those who suffer for the sake of righteousness are blessed not by the persecution itself but because they walk with Christ through the experience. And they experience the blessing of God precisely because they are most like God in these moments. And God takes us in our brokenness and multiplies our ministry through it.

THE BREAD

Jesus blessed the bread. In doing so, He spoke words—creative words. He pronounced words that elevated the bread beyond a simple, common element to something quite special: bread that would multiply and feed a multitude (Matthew 14), bread that would open the eyes of those who had been blind (Luke 24), bread that would impart grace (Mark 14).

Blessed bread becomes special bread. It serves more deeply and widely than an ordinary loaf. It ministers to more people and touches their lives in unexpected ways. It retains the power to be a blessing, even when it is broken. Brokenness does not destroy the bread. On the contrary, it simply extends its reach.

Jesus blessed the bread.

While blessed bread becomes extraordinary, non-blessed bread can never be anything but ordinary. Without the blessing it can feed only a few and in only one way. Without the blessing it lacks creative power. Without the blessing it fails to multiply.

Jesus blessed the bread of the Eucharist. He also blesses us.

Just as His creative words magnified the ministry of the common loaf, so His words do the same in and through us. He takes us, chooses us, and blesses us.[5] When we hear that blessing with the ear of our hearts, we can become a godly blessing to multitudes. Until we hear it, we live in the limitation of the ordinary.

The Father first pronounced the blessing when we made Christ our Lord. *"You are My beloved [child], in You I am well-pleased"* (Mark 1:11 NASB).

When we receive that blessing in the deepest recesses of our being, it changes us and can change the world. Whereas fear once steered our lives, now love takes the wheel. While we once served others to find security, we now serve others out of our security. And the limitations of the past give way to deeper and wider ministry than we ever imagined.

In the blessing we are prepared for the breaking that comes through persecution. And we discover that we have much in common with the eucharistic loaf. And we receive the breaking because we desire Him.

DESIRING GOD

Desiring God and pursuing God forms the foundation for our resilience when we face opposition. The more we yearn for a covenant walk with Him ("righteousness") the more everything else around us fades in significance. The refrain from a popular hymn reminds us that as we turn our eyes upon Jesus, "the things of earth will grow strangely dim in the light of His glory and grace."[6]

Thomas Merton noted that too often we let our troubles rather than our love for Christ preoccupy us. "Do not desire chiefly to be cherished and consoled by God; desire above all to love Him. Do not anxiously desire to have others find consolation in God, but rather help them to love God."[7]

As someone else has said, "We need to quit telling God how big our troubles are and start telling our troubles how big our God is." It's counterintuitive. Our natural inclination is to seek sympathy and understanding. We want others—even God—to recognize our hardship. So we tell our grief to any who will listen. We cry out to God for consolation. But Merton, who understood the dynamics of suffering, redirects our attention completely—to loving God rather than being loved by Him. As long as we remain the centerpiece of our universe, we'll feel the pain of persecution more keenly. When we finally step off the throne of our own hearts and yield to loving Christ more than we love ourselves, then anything we suffer in our pursuit of Him seems a small price to pay.

Will we desire the Father above anything else? Hearts bursting for Him become bold in the face of all obstacles.

When the Sanhedrin summoned Peter and John to stand before them, they surely expected to see two fishermen, intimidated by a night in prison, cowering and compliant. Instead, they encountered confidence and defiance: "Peter and John replied, 'Judge for yourselves whether it is right in God's sight to obey you rather than God. For we cannot help speaking about what we have seen and heard' " (Acts 4:19–20). And then, after receiving some additional threats, Peter and John went out rejoicing and "with great power the apostles continued to testify to the resurrection of the Lord Jesus, and much grace was upon them all" (Acts 4:33).

The early church experienced persecution because they pursued and preached Christ. They endured persecution because they knew at their core that to share in the sufferings of Christ is also to share in His resurrection. Such people, with faith, courage, and boldness, know an inner strength that shakes the world. They are blessed. And they will be blessed when their hope in Christ means eternity with Him. Are we among these believers?

"You're blessed when your commitment to God provokes persecution. The persecution drives you even deeper into God's kingdom" (Matthew 5:10 THE MESSAGE).

SUMMARY STATEMENT

Those who are persecuted because of righteousness find strength because they hold fast to a different set of blessings (spiritual blessings). And as they live "gospel-worthy" lives—willing to die—they make constant choices to pursue the Father and allow brokenness to multiply their ministry. They can lose nothing that matters and are blessed because in Christ they have eternal hope and promise.

Hearts bursting for Christ become bold in the face of all obstacles.

1. How does our earlier definition of *righteousness* as "pursuing God and inner transformation" shape your view of this last beatitude?

2. What might change if we focused more on "every spiritual blessing" rather than "every material blessing"? How can we shift our focus?

3. The chapter states that we live "gospel-worthy" lives only when we are prepared to sacrifice everything for Christ, and we can only reach that point when we have a deep conviction about the resurrection. How embedded in our lives is this theme of resurrection?

4. Dave Jensen's "stimulus—choice—response" model reminds us that when we face persecution or hardship we must take responsibility for our responses. What are some better choices you could make right now in areas where you experience conflict or opposition?

The 2009 movie *The Blind Side* tells the moving and true story of All-American football star Michael Oher. As a teenager, Oher was surviving on his own, virtually homeless, when Leigh Anne Tuohy spotted him on a street in Memphis, Tennessee. Learning that the young black American was one of her daughter's classmates, Leigh Anne insisted that the young man—wearing shorts and a T-shirt in the freezing night air—come out of the cold. Without a moment's hesitation she invited him to spend the night at the Tuohy home. The movie then traces the tender and loving relationship that developed between Michael and the rich white Tuohy family.

In one memorable scene early in the movie, Oher (whom everyone called "Big Mike") sits in the front seat of one of the family cars. Leigh Anne intends on taking him shopping to buy some clothes, since his only change of clothes is an extra shirt he carries in a plastic bag. As she plies him with questions about his background and what he likes, he retreats within himself. Finally, in exasperation, when she cannot find out what "Big Mike" likes, she says, "Then tell me something you *don't* like!" The timid young giant looks her in the eye and says, "I don't like to be called 'Big Mike.' " Leigh Anne pauses a moment and says, "Okay, Michael. Where shall we shop?" That seemingly small change produced a significant turning point in the relationship.[1]

We bless one another when we hear one another, and when we respect the feelings and dignity of one another.

As Jesus sat down to deliver his famous Sermon on the Mount, a crowd gathered around Him. But they were not nameless strangers. Jesus had evidently listened to some of their stories, perhaps knew some of them quite personally. He did not write a speech to impress the religious academics of His day. Instead, He delivered words of life and hope for the everyday world; a world marked by brokenness, sadness, humiliation, conflict, and persecution. Jesus did not deliver a theoretical analysis of the political landscape of His time. He spoke blessings. He reminded the hungry and the hurting listeners that they were already blessed in so many ways, and more blessing awaited. He encouraged them and comforted them.

Who can accurately assess the power of a blessing?

Mary Ann Bird's life was transformed by a caring, thoughtful word from her teacher. Janet, one of "the least of these" in the Daybreak community, felt reassured by her priest's affirmation. Raymond's father, distraught at his son's accident, found that blessing others softened his own heart toward reconciliation. Pastor Kevin quietly enriched the lives of hundreds of folk who received his cards of encouragement over the years—words that gave life. Mike, desperate to find meaning in life, was delivered from suicide because of a courageous word shared with him by a young street evangelist. An anonymous old woman helped inspire the Greensboro Four and a civil rights movement with a single statement of encouragement. Thomas Powell prepared the soul of a dying young student, Elizabeth DiNunzio, by telling her how much she was loved. And Tom Hagan inspired the demoralized ghetto-dwellers in Port-au-Prince by affirming their worth.[2]

Wherever we turn, words make the difference. And Jesus' words make the greatest difference of all.

CREATING A NEW REALITY

The Beatitudes do not lay out a new set of regulations—things we must do, commands we must keep. On the contrary, they represent words of grace and blessing.

Henri Nouwen once wrote, "I am increasingly aware of how much we fearful, anxious, insecure human beings are in need of a blessing. Children need to be blessed by their parents and parents by their children. We all need each other's blessings."[3]

In a world more familiar with criticism and accusations, abounding in harshness and hurt, and awash in gossip and hostility, we may struggle to hear the blessings. After all, the feeling of being accused and accursed comes easily. We steadily come to believe the inner voice that calls us evil, worthless, ugly, useless, and undeserving. Those words—lies from the pit of hell— become truth to us. We empower them by believing them. How important, then, that we hear and receive the real truth. And that we tell and speak the real truth to others.

> *We empower lies by believing them. How important, then, that we hear and receive the real truth.*

To give a blessing is to create the reality of which it speaks. We ought not to confuse it with empty flattery or vain compliments, sometimes designed to manipulate someone in order to gain something. Quite the contrary, a blessing has only one motive—to build up the other person. And it need not be complicated or sophisticated.[4]

One evening in early 2010, my youngest son, Joel, and I found ourselves sitting at the breakfast bar at home—alone. His mom and older brother Caleb had rushed out the door to get Caleb to an event. And there the two of us sat, finishing up our meal. Joel was quiet for a moment, then said, "Dad, let's have a man-to-man talk!" *Uh-oh.* What could that mean? What was on his mind? Would this be one of those golden opportunities to share some life wisdom? "Okay, mate,"

I said. "What would you like to chat about?" Joel hesitated, glanced around a little awkwardly, and then replied, "I don't know. Anything you like."

My ten-year-old was not seeking the wisdom of the ages or any deep insight. He simply wanted relationship. The specific words mattered little to him. What mattered far more was my willingness to speak with intimacy: man-to-man.

Blessings are like that. We may feel that we could never speak blessings because we could never find the right words. But the right words are any words that we speak tenderly and lovingly person-to-person. Blessings are a function of the heart more than the mouth. Yet how can we develop more life-giving speech?

SOME STEPS FORWARD

1. LOOK FOR THE BEST IN PEOPLE. GIVE THEM A FREE UPGRADE.

A friend once asked me how many good friends I had. I hesitated, wondering how many of my fingers and toes I might need. I started to mumble about lots of connections, acquaintances, and colleagues but not so many good friends.

"Why not give everyone a free upgrade?" he asked.

Blessings are a function of the heart more than the mouth.

Why not? Grace would offer everyone the free upgrade whether they ask for it or not and perhaps let them grow into the relationship. That's what Jesus did. Shortly before His crucifixion He declared to the disciples, "I have called you friends" (John 15:15). And He generously included Judas (soon to betray Him), Peter (soon to deny Him), and all the other disciples (soon to abandon Him).

Perhaps that's what Jesus had in mind when He said, "Love your enemies" (Matthew 5:44). We offer a free upgrade, whether it's received or not, because that's what the Father offers us every day. We look past the foibles and failures of others and refuse to let their weaknesses (or our own) define our relationship. Even more than that, we choose to see their strengths—and to bless them.

What might happen if we upgraded each other as readily as the Father upgrades us from strangers to family and from enemies to sons and daughters? What might happen if we blessed each other as readily as the Father blesses us?

Grace. No strings attached. A free upgrade. It provides a great foundation for a lifestyle of blessing others.

2. Speak words of affirmation, not criticism.

Once we commit ourselves to *seeing* people in a positive light, we then begin to *speak* to them in a positive way. The words we speak are always an overflow of the heart. Jesus reminds us:

> Out of the overflow of the heart the mouth speaks. The good man brings good things out of the good stored up in him, and the evil man brings evil things out of the evil stored up in him. (Matthew 12:34–35)

Once we upgrade everyone in our hearts, we can perhaps at last lay aside our usual tendency to criticize and begin to affirm them.

The word of affirmation need not be effusive. We don't have to go over the top or suddenly start passing out false compliments. By now we should know that blessings are usually gentle, simple, and heartfelt. "Have a great day" might be a small blessing (and a major step up) in our relationship with some people. "You're a good man, Joe" can be a meaningful and touching blessing (if someone is a man and his name is Joe). Start in simple and small ways, and watch the changes. Our words of affirmation help produce the upgrades that we have quietly awarded people in our hearts.

3. PRaiSe others.

The word *praise* provides a helpful framework for speaking bless-ings. If we make an acrostic of the consonants (*P, R,* and *S*) it can remind us of several key elements.

First, remember the *P* and make your blessing *Personal.* A bless-ing spoken to a crowd or a group has quite a different impact than a blessing spoken one-on-one. Both are valid, but the personal blessing evokes a significantly different response. We make it personal, in part, by using someone's name. Consider the difference between "Hey, man, you're cool!" and "Greg, you make a real difference in my life."

Names matter a lot in the Bible because they matter a lot to the Father. So much so that in eternity we won't simply be a nameless mass of folk gathered around the throne of God. Rather, He will give each of us a new name. In the letters to the seven churches recorded in Revelation, the Lord declares:

> To him who overcomes, I will give some of the hidden manna. I will also give him a white stone with a *new name* written on it, known only to him who receives it. (Revelation 2:17)

> He who overcomes . . . I will never blot out *his name* from the book of life, but will acknowledge *his name* before my Father and his angels. (Revelation 3:5)

> Him who overcomes . . . I will write on him *the name* of my God and *the name* of the city of my God, the new Jerusalem, which is coming down out of heaven from my God; and I will also write on him *my new name.* (Revelation 3:12)

Names matter. Blessings touch people most deeply when we per-sonalize them. "Mary, your thoughtfulness is a gift to everyone." "Matt, you're a great kid." "Jeff, you have a heart the size of a watermelon." Make your blessing personal. Use names.

Second, consider the *R* and make your blessing *Random.*

Random blessings touch us far more deeply than planned ones. When a pastor closes a service with a blessing for the congregation (which is highly appropriate but neither personal nor random) we appreciate it and receive it gratefully. But when the boss comes unexpectedly into our cubicle or office at work and says, "Kim, you're an

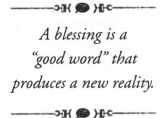

A blessing is a "good word" that produces a new reality.

excellent worker," we receive it quite differently. When we surprise our kids with a random blessing (remember, a blessing is a "good word" that produces a new reality) it makes a difference to them too. If we only build them up when they win something or bring home a decent report card, we're missing the boat. How about randomly saying to that kid you coach on the basketball team, "Josh, you have a kind spirit, and I'm proud of you"? When we randomly bless people in our lives, we exponentially add to the power of the blessing.

Finally, build in the *S* and make your blessing *Specific*.

We're inclined to make blessings generic, but their power grows when they become specific. We might say to a co-worker, "Mandy, you're a good friend," and it will touch her heart at one level. But it moves to a deeper place when we say, "Mandy, your prayers and kind words give me such encouragement. Bless you." A specific blessing is the richest kind, even if it's to say, "God bless you with peace and grace during this season of heartache." We invoke a particular blessing from the Lord.[5]

The combination of personal, random, and specific elements in our blessing of others will have dramatic consequences for both us and those we bless.

WE CAN DO IT

Lutheran pastor and professor Dietrich Bonhoeffer, whom the Nazis killed at the end of World War II for plotting against Hitler, wrote: "With every beatitude the gulf is widened between the disciples and the people."[6] At first glance, it may feel that way for us too. Jesus blesses those who are meek, who hunger and thirst for righteousness, who are merciful, who are pure in heart, and who are persecuted because of righteousness. It feels like an increasingly tall order for us to live up to—until we realize that these Beatitudes are meant to have precisely the opposite effect! Rather than distancing us, Jesus intends these blessings to include us and draw us closer to himself.

It would be easy to nurture a daunted feeling; a sense that we have so far to grow. However, the Beatitudes invite us all into the place of blessing.

The Beatitudes invite us all into the place of blessing.

The poor in spirit—those who feel they have no spiritual heritage, pedigree, or accomplishments to point to—are precisely the ones who know their need for the kingdom of grace. And they find it.

Those who mourn, who grieve because they have lost what they loved dearly, are likewise invited into the kingdom for comfort. Those who grieve most do so because they have loved most. What a blessing.

The meek—whom the world likes to tread on—refuse to assert themselves because they have such supreme confidence in the Father's sovereignty over everything. What blessed faith! And it belongs to the meek.

Those who hunger and thirst for righteousness want nothing more than to enter into a life-giving covenant with God. That's not peculiar, or exceptional. But the Kingdom of God opens up to such people and they find what they're looking for. Blessed hunger!

The merciful, those who refuse to take vengeance or pass judgment, discover that they receive what they give. As they forgive and show grace, they inevitably find themselves being forgiven and shown grace. A blessed way to live.

The pure in heart are not the morally perfect but those who want just one thing: God himself. When (or if) we share this intense desire and focus, we discover that God does not hide but gladly reveals himself. Desire is blessed.

Peacemakers, who regularly get themselves into trouble for standing in the gap, reflect the Son of God himself, and will be called the sons of God. It takes no training to be a peacemaker, but a deep conviction that any of us can have.

And finally, blessed are those who are persecuted because of righteousness—because they seek to walk with God. Could that not be any of us? The pathway to Christ directs us to die to ourselves, to carry our own cross, and to share in the fellowship of His sufferings. As we walk by faith, we find that there's always a cost. But the cost is incomparably small up against the value of knowing Christ Jesus our Lord. Blessed suffering.

These Beatitudes don't isolate us. They invite us—into the Presence and Kingdom of God.

While we honor the capable, the agile, and the competent, Christ blesses us all, and none more so than those who are the broken and the browbeaten, the hurt and the harassed, the ridiculed and the rejected. We discover, in a moment of clarity, that the blessings of life have nothing to do with our circumstances, but rather the state of our hearts. And as we align our hearts increasingly with Christ we encounter Him and, in the words of the apostle Paul, Christ is formed in us (Galatians 4:19).

THE NEXT STEP

Our journey together through this book has repeatedly alluded to transformation. Blessings—good words—create a new reality. Those words have the power to dramatically encourage or wound us. What diligence we must exercise in blessing each other. But we bless each other most sincerely and most powerfully when we first recognize and receive the blessings of the Father in our own lives.

The act of blessing is not about *How to Get Along Better With People*. Nor is it *Things to Say to Get Our Way*. Rather, our words derive from the overflow of the heart. And as our hearts are touched by the love of Christ, our lips speak words that express faith, hope, and love, and produce the same in others. As God's grace grips us, we become vessels of grace to others.

The blessings that we utter, carried along and imbued with power by the Holy Spirit in this mystery we call communication, can change our marriages, our families, and our communities.

But beyond our language, we also experience the blessing of God as we pursue Him, embrace Him, and hold to Him. Donald Bloesch has written: "The key to true piety [and blessing] is not to subscribe to the ethical teachings of Moses or of Jesus, nor is it to have the right ideas about God and reality. Instead it is being united with Christ by faith, then living the kind of life that proceeds from that union."[7] As we live in His Kingdom and carry out the values of Christ, we discover that God repeatedly speaks the greatest blessing of all to us—the one that carries us into and through eternity: "You are My beloved [child], in You I am well-pleased" (Mark 1:11 NASB).

"The grace of the Lord Jesus Christ, and the love of God, and the fellowship of the Holy Spirit, be with you all" (2 Corinthians 13:14 NASB).

Notes

INTRODUCTION

1. Lee Dye, "Study: Negative Words Dominate Language: Why Do Humans Have More Words to Describe the Negative?" *ABC News,* February 2, 2005, *http://abcnews.go.com/Technology/DyeHard/Story?id=460987&page=1.*

2. Peggy Bert, "Positive & Negative Words: Why the 5-to-1 Ratio Works," *Christianity Today,* 2008, *www.christianitytoday.com/mp/2008/spring/7.26.html.*

3. Story told in Thomas G. Long, *Testimony: Talking Ourselves into Being Christian* (San Francisco: Jossey-Bass, 2004), 85–86.

4. Thomas Sweet, "I Wish You Were My Little Girl," January 15, 2006, *www.firstpresjamestown.com/2006Sermons/i_wish_you_were_my_little_girl.htm.*

5. The ancient writer of Proverbs forcefully describes the power of words: "Death and life are in the power of the tongue" (18:21 KJV); "a soft tongue breaks the bone" (25:15 NASB); "a gentle tongue is a tree of life, but perverseness in it breaks the spirit" (15:4 ESV).

6. David Silver, "The Meaning of the Word 'Shalom,'" *http://therefinersfire.org/meaning_of_shalom.htm,* notes the extended meaning of *shalom* as "completeness, wholeness, health, peace, welfare, safety, soundness, tranquility, prosperity, perfectness, fullness, rest, harmony, the absence of agitation or discord."

7. For example, consider Jacob, who called together his sons and pronounced his blessings (Genesis 49:1–27). The account concludes: "All these are the twelve tribes of Israel, and this is what their father said to them when he blessed them, giving each the blessing appropriate to him" (v. 28). Interestingly, by contrast, when we gather around the bedside of the dying, it is usually to say good-bye but not to receive (or impart) blessings.

8. Parker Palmer, *To Know As We Are Known* (San Francisco: Harper & Row, 1993), 44–45.

9. Jacques Ellul, trans. by Joyce Main Hanks, *The Humiliation of the Word* (Grand Rapids, MI: Eerdmans, 1985), 155–156.

10. Brennan Manning, *The Ragamuffin Gospel* (Sisters, OR: Multnomah, 1990, 2000), 14–15.

11. Andrej Kodjak, *A Structural Analysis of the Sermon on the Mount* (New York: Walter de Gruyter, 1987).

12. These blessings are often called the *Beatitudes*. This latter term is simply taken from the Latin word *beatus*, which means "blessed" or "happy."

CHAPTER 1

1. Henri J. M. Nouwen, *Life of the Beloved: Spiritual Living in a Secular World* (New York: Crossroad Publishing, 1992), 69–71.

2. The Pharisees formed as a movement sometime in the second century BC based on the assumption that if the people would return to God and obey Him strictly according to the Law, then the Lord would fulfill His promise to give the land to Israel (e.g., Deuteronomy 6:18–19 NASB: "You shall do what is right and good in the sight of the LORD, that it may be well with you and that you may go in and possess the good land which the LORD swore to give your fathers, by driving out all your enemies from before you, as the LORD has spoken"). Israel's "exile" within its own land could end only with strict obedience. Thus the Pharisees no doubt saw themselves as the ultimate patriots.

3. The Sermon on the Plain in Luke 6:20–49 has similarities to the Sermon on the Mount in Matthew 5–7. However, Luke's record of the Beatitudes has quite a different ring: "Blessed are you who are poor. . . . Blessed are you who hunger now. . . . Blessed are you who weep now. . . . Blessed are you when men hate you. . . ." (NASB). Rather than try and reconcile the different terms and tones, this study focuses specifically on the Matthean text.

4. Romans 5:1–2: "Therefore, having been justified *by faith*, we have peace with God through our Lord Jesus Christ, through whom also we have obtained our introduction *by faith* into this grace in which we stand" (NASB).

5. Dallas Willard, *The Divine Conspiracy* (San Francisco: Harper-SanFrancisco, 1998), 98–99.

6. Willard, *The Divine Conspiracy*, 102.

7. Paul Simon's paraphrase in the song "Blessed," 1965.

8. Manning, *The Ragamuffin Gospel*, 53.

9. Beyond the mere acceptability of the "poor in spirit" we might also note their strategic Kingdom usefulness. Eugene Peterson writes: "The men and women who are going to be most valuable to us in spiritual formation-by-resurrection are most likely going to be people at the edge of respectability: the poor, minorities, the suffering, the rejected, poets, and children." *Living the Resurrection* (Colorado Springs, CO: NavPress, 2006), 26.

10. Dorothy Day, *The Long Loneliness* (New York: HarperCollins, 1952), 199.

11. John Stott, *Christian Counter-Culture* (Leicester, England: Inter-Varsity Press, 1978), 31. Stott also makes the interesting comparison between the ninefold fruit of the Spirit (Galatians 5:22–23) and the eight Beatitudes that Christ presents.

12. Thomas Merton, *No Man Is an Island* (Boston, MA: Shambhala Library, 1955, 1983, 2005), 248.

13. Merton, *No Man Is an Island*, 24.

CHAPTER 2

1. Sue Mosteller in Wil Hernandez, *Henri Nouwen and Soul Care* (Mahwah, NJ: Paulist Press, 2008), xi.

2. Some grief, of course, may come with the loss of a home or a job or something else over which we've had dominion. In such cases, fear or a sense of injustice may lie behind it.

3. LeRoy Lawson, *Blessed Are We* (Cincinnati, OH: Standard Publishing, 1998), 30.

4. James C. Howell, *The Beatitudes for Today* (Louisville, KY: Westminster John Knox Press, 2006), 42. Wolterstorff's specific quote can be found in Nicholas Wolterstorff, *Lament for a Son* (Grand Rapids, MI: Eerdmans, 1987), 5–6.

5. John Stott (*Christian Counter-Culture*, 34) concludes that these tenses reflect the "now and not yet" of the Kingdom of God. That is, we are blessed now to experience a lesser degree of the promise that we'll be blessed later to experience in full. Perhaps so, but this reads back into the text a heavy dose of later Christian theology. How did the crowd on that first hillside understand it?

6. Robert Frost, "Reluctance," *www.ketzle.com/frost/reluctan.htm.* Frost was born in San Francisco in 1874, and died in 1963, just short of his eighty-ninth birthday, having spent most of his life in New England. "Reluctance" was published in 1913.

7. It's not unusual for commentators to spiritualize the Beatitudes and suggest that this beatitude calls us to grieve over our sin. For example, Cameron Lee writes in *Unexpected Blessing* (Downers Grove, IL: InterVarsity, 2004), 93: "In a culture that is tone-deaf to sin, we mourn to attune our spirits to God's will for the world." Is mourning really the *pathway* to attunement with God or the *expression* of it? Surely Jesus does not beckon us to false tears so that we might develop a true heart.

8. John Stott, *The Beatitudes: Developing Spiritual Character* (Downers Grove, IL: InterVarsity, 1998), 17, asserts: "It is plain from the

context that those Jesus promised comfort are not primarily those who mourn the loss of a loved one, but those who mourn the loss of their innocence, their righteousness, their self-respect. It is not the sorrow of bereavement to which Christ refers, but the sorrow of repentance." Does the context really narrow grief to this element alone? To say that it does seems to force the meaning.

9. Jesus said of the Holy Spirit: "When he comes, he will convict the world of guilt in regard to sin and righteousness and judgment" (John 16:8). When referring to individual lives, theologians call this *prevenient grace*—the grace of God that comes to an individual, convicts them and calls them, before they receive the gracious gift of eternal life.

10. Merton, *No Man Is an Island*, 220.

11. Mother Teresa, *A Simple Path* (New York: Random House, 1995), 46.

12. Dorothy Day, famous twentieth-century Catholic social activist, recounts this comment by Peter Claver in her article "Room for Christ," *The Catholic Worker* (December 1945): 2. See also *www.catholicworker.org/dorothyday/daytext.cfm?TextID=416&SearchTerm=claver,%20Sister%20Peter*.

CHAPTER 3

1. Kevin Harney, "Creating a Culture of Blessing," Pastors.com, *www.pastors.com/blogs/ministrytoolbox/archive/2009/11/18/creating-a-culture-of-blessing.aspx*.

2. At least some of the crowd may have recognized the saying from Psalm 37:9, 11(NASB), where David declared, "Those who wait for the LORD, they will inherit the land. . . . The humble will inherit the land."

3. In the New Testament, we find the other reference to *praus* embedded in Matthew 21:5 (a quotation from Zechariah 9:9). It anticipates the arrival of the coming King as "gentle [meek], and mounted on a donkey" (NASB). A related form of *praus—prautēs*

(noun)—is also found in the New Testament. See 1 Corinthians 4:21 (KJV): "a spirit of meekness"; 2 Corinthians 10:1(KJV): "the meekness . . . of Christ"; Galatians 5:22–23 (KJV): "the fruit of the Spirit . . . meekness"; Colossians 3:12 (KJV): "put on . . . meekness"; Ephesians 4:2 (KJV): "with all lowliness and meekness . . . forbearing one another in love," etc.

4. W. E. Vine, *Vine's Expository Dictionary of Old and New Testament Words* (Iowa Falls, IA: Revell, 1981), 55–56.

5. William Barclay notes that the term *prautēs* was used by the Greek philosopher Aristotle long before Christ. Aristotle squeezed it into his own philosophical model, which identified virtues as the means between extremes. For him, meekness "is the happy medium between too much and too little anger." The Daily Bible Study Series, *The Gospel of Matthew*, Vol 1 (Philadelphia, PA: Westminster Press, 1975), 96.

6. Both of these literary examples are taken from Lynne Truss, *Eats, Shoots & Leaves* (New York: Gotham Books, 2003), 9–10.

7. We usually view people who fail to defend themselves or demand their rights as uneducated, uninformed, weak, or complacent. Folk who take the "lesser" jobs in society—perhaps gardeners, janitors, or house cleaners—get treated as second-class citizens, though they may be entirely content in their vocation.

8. Mother Teresa, *A Simple Path,* xxi.

9. Dan Elliott, "Mayumi Heene Admits Hoax: Balloon Boy's Mother Confesses to Authorities," *The Huffington Post,* October 23, 2009, *www.huffingtonpost.com/2009/10/23/mayumi-heene-admits-hoax_n_332307.html.*

10. A. W. Tozer, *The Pursuit of God* (Camp Hill, PA: Christian Publications, 1993), 109.

11. Stott, *Christian Counter-Culture,* 43.

12. David Benner, *The Gift of Being Yourself* (Downers Grove, IL: InterVarsity, 2004), 76–77.

13. This excerpt from an email received in October 2009 is used with permission.

CHAPTER 4

1. This story is based on an email to me from Mike Nolan in September 2009. Mike is a former student of mine. His story is used with permission.

2. Antiquities 17.2.4. See University of Rochester Web site: *www.pas.rochester.edu/~tim/study/Pharisees.pdf.*

3. While the issue of *self-righteousness* will not be a theme of this chapter, it deserves a mention here. We can easily slip into comparing our faith and efforts against those around us. Such pride breeds nothing but division and self-delusion. The righteousness of which Jesus speaks in this beatitude is a complete contrast to self-righteousness.

4. We find a good example of this midway through the Sermon on the Mount, when Jesus says, "If your right hand causes you to sin, cut it off" (Matthew 5:30). We all know that cutting off a hand does not reduce feelings of anger or violence. The statement is an exaggeration to drive home the seriousness of the underlying message.

5. For example, "If anyone comes to me and does not hate his father and mother, his wife and children, his brothers and sisters—yes, even his own life—he cannot be my disciple" (Luke 14:26).

6. The making of this covenant is described in Genesis 31.

7. Many years later, the Lord changed Abram's name to Abraham as a prophetic gesture that the childless man would become the "father of a multitude" (the meaning of the name *Abraham*). See Genesis 17:5.

8. Later, under the Mosaic covenant, righteousness became associated with law-keeping—keeping the rules. This is sometimes called forensic (or moral) righteousness. But according to the apostle

Paul, Abraham serves as the model for righteousness by faith of which Jesus spoke, best called "covenant righteousness." "Even so, Abraham believed God, and it was reckoned to him as righteousness" (Galatians 3:6 NASB). That is, Abraham is righteous because he fulfilled the covenant term prescribed by God: "Believe."

9. Romans 1:17 affirms that "the righteousness of God is revealed from faith to faith" (NASB). That is, our decision to trust God (and therefore obey His leading) is enough to establish covenant with God.

10. Willard, *The Divine Conspiracy*, 145.

11. Ibid.

12. Scot McKnight equates *righteousness* with *justice* and writes: "What is 'right' is determined by the twin exhortation to love God (by following Jesus) and to love others. For Jesus, justice [righteousness] is about restoring people and society to the love of God and love of others." See *The Jesus Creed: Loving God, Loving Others* (Brewster, MA: Paraclete Press, 2007), 145–146.

13. Tozer, *The Pursuit of God*, 40.

14. Ibid., 38.

15. Frank Laubach, *Letters by a Modern Mystic* (Colorado Springs: Purposeful Design Publications, 2007), 13, 67.

16. Lee, *Unexpected Blessing*, 109.

17. Ibid., 108.

18. See Psalms 6:3; 13:1; 79:5; 89:46.

19. Tozer, *The Pursuit of God*, 30.

20. Calvin Miller, *A Hunger for the Holy* (West Monroe, LA: Howard Publishing, 2003), 64.

21. Tozer, *The Pursuit of God*, 22.

22. D. Martyn Lloyd-Jones, *Studies in the Sermon on the Mount* (Grand Rapids, MI: Eerdmans, 1979), 75.

23. The apostle Paul writes, "But [the Lord] said to me, 'My grace is sufficient for you, for my power is made perfect in weakness.' Therefore I will boast all the more gladly about my weaknesses, so that Christ's power may rest on me" (2 Corinthians 12:9).

CHAPTER 5

1. Walter Lüthi and Robert Brunner reacted against this and concluded that "the kind heart that we may have inherited from our mother or our grandfather is a very questionable thing. A kind heart is often a culpably weak heart" (*The Sermon on the Mount* [Edinburgh, UK: Oliver & Boyd, 1963], 15). Interestingly, these two German theologians wrote their original work in 1936, during the rise of the Nazi regime.

2. See *www.merriam-webster.com/dictionary/mercy.*

3. This portion of Shakespeare's *The Merchant of Venice* appears in William J. Bennett, *The Book of Virtues* (Melbourne, Australia: Bookman Press, 1993), 151–152. I have slightly modified Shakespeare's classic text to make it more readable and understandable.

4. For example, on one occasion as Jesus passed by a man who had been blind from birth, His disciples asked Him, "Rabbi, who sinned, this man or his parents, that he was born blind?" (John 9:2). Additionally, consider the story in Mark 2:1–12, where Jesus heals a paralytic. He says to the man, "Son, your sins are forgiven" (v. 5), which sparks a firestorm among the scribes who are sitting there. They believe that sickness and sin are connected, but if Jesus could forgive this man's sins, then He clearly has divine power. Mercy, not just compassion, led to healing.

5. See Richard Wurmbrand, "With My Own Eyes," http://*kmknapp .blogspot.com/2004/07/great-mystery-of-forgiveness.html.*

6. This represents an extraordinary difference between the message

of Jesus and the teaching of the Old Testament. Scot McKnight notes: "Forgiveness doesn't appear in any of Moses' lists of commandments. In all the prayers of David, we don't find the prayers concerned with forgiving one another. And the prophets don't call Israelites to forgive one another." In fact, "Forgiveness is generally granted in the Old Testament *on the condition of repentance.*" See *The Jesus Creed: Loving God, Loving Others*, 218–219. Jesus, however, blesses the merciful and calls us to the kind of mercy that forgives unconditionally.

7. There is, of course, another element to this. We may well think of people as our "enemies" who do not consider themselves such. Mercy may also demand of us that we move past prejudice, racism, and biases to love all people sincerely. Frank Laubach, well-known twentieth-century missionary to the Philippines, had a divine revelation on Signal Hill, behind his home in the Philippines. He wrote: "My lips began to move, and it seemed to me that God was speaking. 'My child,' my lips said, 'you have failed because you do not really love these Moros. You feel superior to them because you are white. If you can forget that you are an American and think only how I love them, they will respond.' " Laubach had to confront prejudice within himself, despite his commitment to these people as a missionary! See Frank C. Laubach, *Forty Years with the Silent Billion* (Old Tappan, NJ: Revell, 1970), 421.

8. Sheldon Vanauken, *A Severe Mercy* (New York: HarperOne, 1987), 211.

9. Ibid., 216.

10. Consider Exodus 33:5: "The LORD had said to Moses, 'Tell the Israelites, "You are a stiff-necked people. If I were to go with you even for a moment, I might destroy you. Now take off your ornaments and I will decide what to do with you." ' "

CHAPTER 6

1. For details of this story, see Martha Waggoner, "Protesters reflect

on success of 1960s sit-ins at segregated lunch counters," *The Intelligencer*, January 31, 2010, *www.cleveland.com/nation/index .ssf/2010/01/protesters_reflect_on_success.html*, on the 50th anniversary of the event. The elderly white woman's words of encouragement can be found in Michele Norris's article, "The Woolworth Sit-In That Launched a Movement," *www.npr.org/templates/story/ story.php?storyId=18615556*. Rosa Parks' famous arrest for refusing to give up her bus seat to a white man happened in Montgomery, Alabama, on December 1, 1955, and sparked the famous Montgomery Bus Boycott about four years before this event.

2. Willard, *The Divine Conspiracy*, 118.

3. Søren Kierkegaard, *Purity of Heart Is to Will One Thing* (New York: Harper Torchbooks, 1956), 206.

4. Tozer, *The Pursuit of God*, 90.

5. Ibid., 83.

6. Thomas à Kempis, ed., William C. Creasy, *The Imitation of Christ* (Notre Dame, IN: Ave Maria Press, 2001), 126. Thomas lived 1380–1471, and some believe that *The Imitation of Christ* represents his editorial work on Gerhard Groote's diary (1340–1384). In any case, *The Imitation of Christ* has become one of the greatest classics in Christian literature.

7. See *www.cdc.gov/nchs/fastats/divorce.htm*.

8. Lee, *Unexpected Blessing*, 85–86.

9. Waggoner, "Protesters reflect on success of 1960s sit-ins."

CHAPTER 7

1. Liz Robbins, "Collision Course," *Runner's World* (January 2010): 84–91.

2. Quoted in *Context* (April 1, 1993): 6.

3. See John Dear, *A Persistent Peace: One Man's Struggle for a Nonviolent*

World (Chicago: Loyola Press, 2008). This autobiography highlights the personal hazards of Dear's own peacemaking.

4. The entire text of the speech and the text of many other significant historical speeches can be found in *Speeches That Changed the World* (London, UK: Murdoch Books, 2005).

5. This phrase *sons of God* has significant Old Testament associations. In the Psalms, the king of Israel is considered a son of God. See Psalm 2:7: "You are my Son; today I have become your Father"; and Psalm 72:1: "Endow the king with your justice, O God, the royal son with your righteousness"; and Psalm 82:6: "I said, 'You are "gods"; you [rulers] are all sons of the Most High.' " Thus to say that the peacemakers will be called the sons of God is also to say that they shall rule.

6. The powerful story is retold in Donald Kraybill, Steven Nolt, and David Weaver-Zercher, *Amish Grace: How Forgiveness Transcended Tragedy* (San Francisco: John Wiley & Sons, 2007). It may seem odd, at first, that the Amish should forgive Mrs. Roberts. What had she done? But the guilt that she felt for not having stopped her husband or even seen this violence rising in him was a guilt needing forgiveness.

7. Max Lucado, *You Are Special* (Wheaton, IL: Crossway Books, 1997), 31.

8. Consider, for example, such labels as *terrorist, militant, insurgent,* and *enemy combatant.* These terms remove the human face and story from consideration and make it far easier to hate and kill.

9. CBS News Report, "Woman Shoots Intruder During 9-1-1 Call," December 9, 2009. *www.cbsnews.com/stories/2009/12/09/earlyshow/main5949873.shtml?tag=contentMain;contentBody.*

10. Michael Peck, "Why the Army Doesn't Train on Xboxes," Danger Room, February 9, 2010, *www.wired.com/dangerroom/2010/02/why-the-army-doesnt-train-on-xboxes.* The author notes the Army's use of video game–like software to train its soldiers. Our entertainment has become the military's training tools—or vice versa.

11. John Woolman, *The Journal and Major Essays of John Woolman,* ed., Phillips P. Moulton (Richmond, IN: Friends United Press, 1971), 85.

12. Ibid., 84.

13. CBS News, "Man Exonerated after 35 Years behind Bars," December 17, 2009, *www.cbsnews.com/stories/2009/12/17/national/main5991535.shtml.*

CHAPTER 8

1. Tom Hagan, "I Am Humbled by These People," *National Catholic Reporter,* February 1, 2010, *http://ncronline.org/news/global/i-am-humbled-these-people.*

2. The terms *Kingdom of God* and *Kingdom of heaven* have often been viewed as interchangeable. However, the two phrases speak to different issues. *Kingdom of God* focuses on whose kingdom it is, while *Kingdom of the heavens* (literally) expresses the extent of the Kingdom. See my *Living the Lord's Prayer* (Minneapolis, MN: Bethany House, 2008), 66.

3. For an insightful critique of the prosperity gospel, see John Piper's online video upload "Why I Abominate the Prosperity Gospel," *www.youtube.com/watch?v=jLRue4nwJaA.*

4. Speaking to preachers, A. W. Tozer wrote: "I think it highly improbable that anyone who speaks cautiously can speak effectively. His timidity will deactivate his effort and render it impotent. It is true that the church has suffered from pugnacious men who would rather fight than pray, but she has suffered more from timid preachers who would rather be nice than be right. The latter have done more harm, if for no other reason than that there are so many more of them" in *God Tells the Man Who Cares* (Camp Hill, PA: Christian Publications, 1992), 131.

5. Henri Nouwen wrote a wonderful book that explores this bread-breaking meal motif (taken, blessed, broken, given) as a pattern for our own lives and discipleship. See Henri Nouwen, *Life of the*

Beloved: Spiritual Living in a Secular World (New York: Crossroad Publishing, 2002). See also Eugene Peterson, *Living the Resurrection*, 80–83.

6. Helen Lemmel wrote the popular hymn "Turn Your Eyes Upon Jesus" in 1918 after a missionary friend gave her a tract entitled "Focused." For more of the backstory to this popular hymn see *http://articles.christiansunite.com/article6029.shtml.*

7. Merton, *No Man Is an Island*, 270.

FINAL REFLECTIONS

1. The film was based on the true story by Michael Lewis, *The Blind Side: Evolution of a Game* (New York: W. W. Norton & Co., 2007). Michael Oher, born May 28, 1986, repeated both first and second grades and attended eleven different schools during his first nine years as a student. Following the healing and restorative intervention of the Tuohy family, he finished high school and went on to play college football with the University of Mississippi. He graduated with a degree in criminal justice in the spring of 2009, and the Baltimore Ravens drafted him in the first round of the 2009 NFL draft with a five-year, $13.8 million contract.

2. These statements refer to the stories that open each of the chapters in the book.

3. Nouwen, *Life of the Beloved*, 68.

4. Eugene Peterson frames this wonderfully for the pastor: "What pastors do, or at least are called to do, is really quite simple. We say the word *God* accurately, so that congregations of Christians can stay in touch with the basic realities of their existence, so they know what is going on . . . so they will recognize and respond to the God who is both on our side and at our side when it doesn't seem like it and we don't feel like it." Eugene Peterson, *Under the Unpredictable Plant: An Exploration in Vocational Holiness* (Grand Rapids, MI: Eerdmans, 1992), 172.

5. This invocation of God is what distinguishes a blessing from

a simple compliment. Calvin Miller notes, "Compliments are the parents of egotism, and egotism seldom stops celebrating its own power long enough to marvel at God's." See *A Hunger for the Holy,* 46.

6. Quoted in John Stott, *Sermon on the Mount: 13 Studies for Individuals or Groups* (Downers Grove, IL: InterVarsity Press, 1987), 15.

7. Donald G. Bloesch, *Faith and Its Counterfeits* (Downers Grove, IL: InterVarsity Press, 1981), 19.

DAVID TIMMS teaches New Testament and Theology and serves as chair of the Graduate Ministry Department at Hope International University in Fullerton, California. Australian by birth, David has been a church planter, pastor, and trainer of pastors for twenty-five years. He publishes an e-zine, *In Hope,* that shares his reflections on Christian leadership and spiritual formation. He and his wife, Kim, have three sons and live in Fullerton, California.

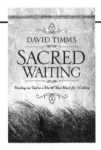

DATE DUE
